Presented to:

_____

From:

_____

The Freedom Answer Book

How the Government Is Taking Away Your Constitutional Freedoms

Judge Andrew P. Napolitano

THOMAS NELSON
Since 1798

NASHVILLE   DALLAS   MEXICO CITY   RIO DE JANEIRO

Published in Nashville, Tennessee, by Thomas Nelson®. Thomas Nelson is a registered trademark of Thomas Nelson, Inc.

Cover design by LeftCoast Design, Portland, OR 97225

Typeset by Thinkpen Design, Inc., www.thinkpendesign.com

Thomas Nelson, Inc., titles may be purchased in bulk for educational, business, fund-raising, or sales promotional use. For information, please e-mail SpecialMarkets@ThomasNelson.com.

ISBN-13: 978-1-4003-2029-5

Printed in China

12 13 14 15 [WAI] 5 4 3 2 1

www.thomasnelson.com

This book includes material from *Constitution in Exile,*
*It Is Dangerous to Be Right When the Government
Is Wrong,* and *Constitutional Chaos.*

Contents

Foreword

The world in the 21st century may not really be more complicated than in the past, but it certainly is more confusing. Not so long ago—in 2008—we had a president (George W. Bush) who proclaimed, "I've abandoned free-market principles to save the free-market system." Huh? Bush then diverted funds from the Troubled Asset Relief Program (TARP) that was supposed to shore up the nation's financial system to bail out GM and Chrysler, an action that was not only economically dubious but legally questionable.

More recently, we've had a president (Barack Obama) who has defended his right to kill American citizens he thinks are threats to the republic without having to consult either Congress or the courts; what's more, Obama has said such actions are "humane" because the preferred method of execution—strikes by unmanned drones—are less likely than regular bombing raids to include collateral damage. Only slightly less troubling was one of his administration's lawyers admitting that the government has the right to force citizens to purchase broccoli in the pursuit of health care reform. But that's what Elena Kagan did during her 2010 Senate confirmation hearings for the Supreme Court, where she now sits.

Forget the Founding Fathers—our *grandfathers* couldn't have imagined the world in which we live (and they could remember such fast-and-loose presidents as FDR, LBJ, and Richard Nixon). Politicians and other powerful individuals and groups at the very highest levels of U.S. society routinely abuse the legal system and historical precedent for their own purposes and to further their own ends. Such folks are often clever rhetoricians and they always work hard to make their positions seem eminently sensible, attractive, and legally sound.

In a world in which murder is humane and capitalism can be saved only by abandoning it, Judge Andrew Napolitano isn't simply the most electrifying, ubiquitous, and insistent defender of liberty in print and on screen, he is a model of engagement, decorum, and principle. As someone who has learned new insights and been exposed to new outrages with every one of his articles, books, and appearances, I'm overwhelmed with gratitude that he is fighting not just the good fight but the great fight. If we preserve—and as important, expand—the scope of free individuals to live their lives according to their own lights and talents, it will be due in part to the efforts of the Judge and the people he inspires. Whether he's talking about the horrible legacy of the *Dred Scott* decision, the glorious legacy of Jackie Robinson, the need for constitutional protections especially for defendants already convicted in the court of public opinion, or historical precedents for limiting state power, he's never less than directly on point and completely convincing.

Yes, it's a confusing world, all right. But much less so because the Judge is out there, fighting for all of us and all our rights. *The Freedom Answer Book* is culled from the best of his published work. It takes complicated legal theory and history and breaks it down so anyone and everyone can understand the freedoms we possess and what it takes to defend them. It's not just a great read (like all of the Judge's work), it's an essential read for every citizen who wants to make sure they can cut through the self-serving rhetoric and actions of politicians and other powerful people who want to take away our rights to life, liberty, and the pursuit of happiness.

Nick Gillespie

Nick Gillespie is editor in chief of Reason.com
and co-author of *The Declaration of Independents: How
Libertarian Politics Can Fix What's Wrong with America*

Constitutional Basics: Laying the Foundation

The Constitution of the United States is the most examined and debated document in our country's history. It was written as a classic American compromise after months of debate at the Constitutional Convention in Philadelphia, which met during the summer of 1787. Essentially, the document constructs, establishes, and imposes limitations on the federal government by which each of the states gave some of their independent sovereign power away and created a new central government.

The first effort for creating a federal government was the Articles of Confederation. Basically it created an umbrella government, subject to the wishes of the various states, any one of which could disregard a law that the central government enacted. Because of fears that Great Britain, the country from which our colonies broke away, would someday attempt to take back the states—fears which, of course, came true in 1812—many political leaders felt the Articles of Confederation did not provide the type of central government strong enough to unite the former colonies into one sovereign capable of dealing with all foreign governments with one voice, and strong enough to protect its people.

The Constitution is unique because it indisputably establishes the primacy of the individual over the state. It guarantees liberties and guarantees that the central government will not impair them. Basically, the Constitution is the result of a compromise between federalists personified by Alexander Hamilton, who wanted a very strong central government, and anti-federalists personified by Thomas Jefferson, who wanted strict limitations on the new government's powers and guarantees of liberty. Thus, out of that conflict of ideas, the federal government was born.

The Constitution provides for a strong chief executive—not a king—but an executive who is not subject to either of the two branches. What do I mean by this? In the modern European system, the head of the government is the prime minister. The prime minister is also the head of the political party that dominates the legislative branch. The prime minister of most modern European countries is not elected in a popular vote. His party's representatives are elected to parliament, and if they have a majority in parliament, they choose him as the leader of their party to become the leader of the government. The prime minister's name does not appear on a national ballot as a candidate for that office.

Here in the US, of course, the president, though voted for popularly, actually is chosen by electors from the states where the voters chose him. The people vote in each state directly for electors, and the electors promise they will cast their state's electoral votes for the winner of that state's popular vote. The person who wins the national popular vote becomes president. Nevertheless, the Constitution gives us a strong chief executive, not one whose powers derive from the legislature, but one whose powers derive from the Constitution. If a British prime minister loses a vote of confidence, that is, if Parliament rejects one of his proposals, he can be swept from office and forced to stand for reelection; not so with the American president. Not only may he lose a vote in the Congress and still keep his job, but he doesn't even have to be in the same party as that which dominates Congress, and frequently that has been the case.

The Congress was created by the Constitution to represent the states and the people. Originally, senators were not popularly elected, but rather elected by state legislatures for six-year terms. Thus, the senators didn't represent the people in a state; they represented the state itself, its government, its sovereignty, in the United States Senate. In 1913, the Constitution was amended to provide for direct popular election of senators.

Members of the House of Representatives have always been popularly elected. The House has always been considered "the people's house," and its representatives seek reelection every two years.

Thus, in the two popular branches of government, we see a classic American compromise. In the Senate are representatives of the sovereign states. In the House of Representatives are representatives of the people. In the presidency is a person who must have broad popular support but could actually be elected without it.

The most peculiar and least understood branch of the American government is the judiciary. The judicial branch of the government consists of life-tenured judges appointed by the president and confirmed by the Senate. These judges, of course, never have to seek election and can only be removed from office upon impeachment, after conviction of a felony.

The purpose of the judicial branch, as created by the Constitution, was to hear trials and apply federal laws to the unique cases before them. In the very famous case of *Marbury v. Madison*, however, in 1803, the Supreme Court decided that its purpose would be grander than that. The Court claimed for itself the power to invalidate acts of the Congress that were inconsistent with the Constitution. At the time, such power was considered a radical notion.

William Marbury had been appointed as a federal magistrate by outgoing President John Adams, a Federalist. His appointment was confirmed by the Senate, but the secretary of state in the Adams administration neglected to give Marbury his formal commission. After Thomas Jefferson, an Anti-Federalist, became president, his secretary of state, James Madison, refused to deliver Marbury his commission. So Marbury sued Madison in the Supreme

Court seeking an order to compel Madison to deliver the commission to Marbury. The Supreme Court rejected Marbury's claim, not because he was not entitled to it (he was), but because the Congressional statute under which he sued, which gave the Supreme Court original jurisdiction over this type of lawsuit, was unconstitutional. This was so, the Court ruled, because the Constitution dictates the areas over which the Supreme Court has original jurisdiction, and the Congress cannot alter that. The party that immediately benefited by the outcome of *Marbury v. Madison* was the Anti-Federalists, who were in power at the time, and the result—that Mr. Marbury did not become a magistrate—was then popular. But of course this power would dog presidents and congresses even up to the present day.

The power is called "judicial review," and it is now universally accepted that not only the Supreme Court, but all federal judges, can review and void acts of Congress or acts of the president that the federal judge is able to demonstrate are inconsistent with the Constitution. For example, if the president were to declare that he did not need to seek reelection and he was entitled to retain his job for life, and a lawsuit were filed challenging that declaration, it would be easy for a federal judge to invalidate the declaration because it is inconsistent with the Constitution, which sets the president's term at four years. If Congress were to enact a law that made it unlawful to criticize members of the Congress, it would be easy for a federal judge to invalidate that law as inconsistent with the First Amendment to the Constitution, which guarantees freedom of speech.

Judicial review is indeed controversial, but it is now nearly universally accepted. Sometimes we call the exercise of judicial review "judicial *activism*" when we disagree with what the Court does; sometimes we call it "judicial *heroism*" when we agree with the judicial outcome.

The amendments to the Constitution are divided into two categories. The first ten of them are known as the Bill of Rights.

The Bill of Rights was promised to Thomas Jefferson and the Anti-Federalists as a condition for their support of the Constitution. The great fear of the Anti-Federalists—those who, if around today, would fear big government—was that the central government would take personal liberty away from individuals and power away from the states. When the authors of the Constitution guaranteed the Anti-Federalists that the document would contain a Bill of Rights which would spell out the rights and liberties that the Constitution would guarantee and would retain powers for the states, it was an easier sell in those states concerned about personal freedom and limited government.

When we use the term *the Bill of Rights*, we are referring only to the first ten amendments to the Constitution. If you read those ten amendments, you will see that they consist of guaranteeing specific individual rights that the federal government cannot take away, and powers that the states will always keep.

After we fought the Civil War and added the Thirteenth, Fourteenth, and Fifteenth Amendments, the courts began interpreting those, especially the Fourteenth, as meaning that not only can the federal government not interfere with liberties guaranteed in the Bill of Rights, but also, none of the state governments can interfere with them either.

What is State Sovereignty?

The starting point of the Constitution is that the thirteen states that formed the federal government were sovereign and independent states free to go their own way. There was a Continental Congress, of course, in 1776. It had little or no power other than to direct then General George Washington as he waged war against the British. The real political power that existed in 1776 was in the governorship and the legislature of each of the thirteen states.

When those political leaders of those thirteen states agreed that the Articles of Confederation were too weak to allow the country to be perceived as a sovereign unit by foreign countries, each of the states gave away some of their power to form the new central government.

Even though the Constitution begins with "We the people," it was really "We the states" that formed the Constitution. The Constitution itself indicates that it would not come into existence until two-thirds of the thirteen *states* agreed to accept it. So when one thinks of the federal government of the United States of America, one should think of a government with limitations imposed on it by the Constitution and with powers given to it by the various states. This, of course, presumes—historically this is the case—the thirteen original states preceded the existence of the federal government and actually, literally gave away some of their powers so as to form a central government. As an example, before 1789, many states issued their own currency and had their own armies. This obviously is something they cannot do under the Constitution because they gave those powers away to the central, federal government.

What is the Separation of Powers?

The Constitution itself divides power among a president who enforces the laws, a Congress which writes the laws, and a judiciary which interprets the laws. It also, of course, limits the powers of the three branches of government so that they deal with problems that are truly federal in nature. Unfortunately, these limitations have rarely been honored, and throughout the many years of our existence, fanatics and busybodies, do-gooders and collectivists in the congresses have found infamous and duplicitous ways—power-hungry judges in the courts have bent over backward to allow congresses and presidents—to exercise power never contemplated by the Constitution.

Article 1, Section 8 specifically lists only eighteen areas of human behavior over which Congress may legislate, and thus the president may enforce and the courts may interpret. Those areas involve coining money, regulating interstate and foreign commerce, establishing rules of naturalization, establishing post offices and courts, and supporting an army and navy. The power to regulate all other areas of human behavior that the Natural Law (see next section) allows governments to regulate was retained by the states. Despite the strict enumeration of congressional powers, the Congress has exercised powers never granted, enumerated, or delegated to it and has regulated, with the courts' approval, everything from automobile speed limits to the amount of sugar in ketchup, from the size of toilet bowls to the wages of janitors, from the fat content of cheese to the number of lobsters you can catch and the amount of wheat you can grow, from the number of painkillers your physician can prescribe to the amount of income you can keep.

Jefferson and Madison would not be happy with what's become of this vitally important historical document.

Natural Rights vs.
Positivism:
Balancing State
Government with
Federal Government

What is Natural Law?

F or thousands of years philosophers, scholars, judges, lawyers, and ordinary folks have debated and argued over different theories suggesting the sources of human freedom. Though there are many schools of thought addressing these origins, most contemporary legal scholars in the Western world stand behind two principal theories about the origins of freedom: one school, the Natural Law theorists, argues that freedom comes by virtue of being human—from our own nature. The other school, the Positivists, argues that freedom comes from the government.

Natural Law theory teaches that the law extends from human nature, which is created by God. Thus, the Natural Law theory states that because all human beings desire freedom from artificial restraint and because all human beings yearn to be free, our freedoms stem from our nature— from our very humanity—and ultimately from God. St. Thomas Aquinas, the principal modern interpreter of Natural Law, directly contends that because God is perfectly free and humans are created in His image and likeness, our freedoms come from God. The Founders held this same basic view.

Positivism is more or less the opposite of the Natural Law. Under Positivism, the law is whatever the government in power says it is. Positivism requires that all laws be written down and that there are no theoretical or artificial restraints on the ability of a popularly elected government to enact whatever laws it wishes. Carte blanche all the way.

The advantage of Positivism is that, quite literally, the majority always rules and always gets its way, since there are no minority rights to be protected. Thus, if, under a Positivism theory, a state legislature or the Congress were to enact legislation prohibiting public criticism of abortion, or a state governor were to prevent Christians and Jews from worshiping, so long as the legislature was legally elected and so long as the legislature followed its own rules in enacting the legislation and so long as the legislation proscribed criticism of abortion and authorized the governor's behavior, the prohibition on speech and the interference with the free exercise of religion would be the law of the land, and no court could interfere with it. If rights come from government, they can be repealed by government.

Critics of Positivism have argued that it leads to the tyranny of the majority. These critics remind us that Hitler and his Nazi government were popularly elected and, once in power, under the theory of Positivism, passed all sorts of horrific laws, all of which were lawfully enacted. Because there was no Natural Law to protect the minority, these awful laws became the law of the land.

In America, the Declaration of Independence is traditionally referred to as the "anchor of our liberties." It is clearly a Natural Law document since in it Thomas Jefferson argues that our rights to life, liberty, and the pursuit of happiness come not from the government, but from our Creator.

The Constitution of the United States, as well, does not grant rights but rather recognizes their existence, guarantees their exercise, and requires the government to protect them. For example, the First Amendment to the Constitution reads in part, "Congress shall make no law respecting an establishment of religion or prohibiting the free exercise thereof; or abridging the freedom of speech." This clearly implies that the Founders recognized that freedom of religious worship and freedom of speech come from some source other than the Constitution. The First Amendment, thus, is not a grant of rights to the people, but a restriction on government, preventing it from infringing on the rights the people already have. The amendment also implies that not only may Congress not interfere with freedom of speech or the free exercise of religion, but Congress must prevent all who act in the name of the government from interfering with them as well.

> Which philosophy—Natural Law or Positivism—is most prominent in our government today?

The greatest and gravest threat to personal freedom in this country is that the Positivists are carrying the day. Under their sway, the government violates the law while busily passing more legislation to abridge our liberties.

If we wish to survive the near future with our rights intact, we need to understand the size and scope of the threat. We must also understand its true identity: a government that breaks its own laws.

As human history teaches us, many of the most egregious human rights violations have come at the hand of majorities in so-called "advanced" societies:

- For two hundred years a majority of white Americans institutionalized slavery, the ultimate violation of Natural Rights. This majority of voters in the South were white property owners. These people authorized themselves by law to own black people as slaves.
- During World War II democratically elected officials detained (Asian) Japanese-American citizens but not (Caucasian) German-American citizens.
- Perhaps the most extreme example of the tyranny of the majority is abortion: unborn fetuses who cannot partake in the political process are, for the purposes of this discussion, a minority that has been "outvoted." What could constitute more natural yearnings than to be born and to develop into a human being?! Nonetheless, abortion is a widely accepted practice.

— 29 —

Why can the rule of the majority be dangerous and destructive?

Liberty never lasts in a system where all laws are created by a majority vote. As Benjamin Franklin said, "When the people find that they can vote themselves money, that will herald the end of the republic."

As the *Los Angeles Times* stated in a 1992 editorial about California politics at the time, "Democracy is not freedom. Democracy is two wolves and a lamb voting on what to eat for lunch. Freedom comes from the recognition of certain rights which may not be taken, not even by a 99% vote. Those rights are spelled out in the Bill of Rights and in our California Constitution. Voters and politicians alike would do well to take a look at the rights we each hold, which must never be chipped away by the whim of the majority." Amen.

Before I answer that question, consider that it is illegal in Maine to keep up Christmas decorations after January 14. In Connecticut, the only thing worse than jaywalking is doing so on your hands. In North Dakota, ordering beer and pretzels at a bar might make you guilty of a crime. And, my personal favorite, dogcatchers in Denver are required to post notices of impoundment for stray dogs to see.

According to Positivism, laws like those that give dogs an opportunity to avoid the kennel are perfectly valid merely by virtue of being the pronouncement of the government. But isn't there a promise implied by the social contract that the government will pass laws only for certain purposes? Eminent English jurist William Blackstone proclaimed that laws are only permissible when they are "necessary and expedient for the general advantage of the public." *Necessary* means that that law is a sort of last resort in solving whatever problem the government is seeking to remedy. *Expedient* means that those laws directly further the good of innocent individuals. Thus, according to Blackstone, a law that criminalized consuming beer and pretzels together would not be expedient, whereas a law which criminalized consuming beer while driving a car that could cause human injury would.

Why does this requirement of necessity and expediency exist? Because the only reason government exists is to secure our liberty, so when it criminalizes drinking beer and eating pretzels, not only is it infringing upon those liberties, but it is acting outside the scope of its entire purpose. The first requirement that government must abide by in the process of drafting and enacting a law is that the law is necessary to protect the freedom of persons within the jurisdiction of that government.

Positivism's scheme of law relies upon the people obeying law because they are *afraid* of the government, not because those laws are in accord with the Natural Law and therefore just. If we are to live forever in a legal system founded on Positivism, then we can only hope that we will have laws that, coincidentally, happen to be just.

There are many self-evident truths that all rational persons recognize. Some come from human reason (the sun rises, and we need food, shelter, and clothing), and some come from revelation (we have the rights to life, liberty, property, and happiness; it is wrong to lie, cheat, steal, and murder). Some self-evident truths come from reason and revelation (government is essentially the negation of liberty; humans have free immortal souls while governments are finite and based on coercion and force).

This concept of self-evident truths—or truisms—is absolutely essential to freedom. Why? Because truisms reject both moral relativism and American exceptionalism. Truisms compel an understanding of the laws of nature that animate and regulate all human beings at all times, in all places, and under all circumstances. Therefore truisms equal *freedom*.

The Third Reich provides a case study in how governments devise policies and institutions that trespass on just about every human yearning there is. It is wrong to detain, torture, and murder humans, because they possess an inherent inclination to roam the world freely, to avoid pain, and to preserve their lives. Compulsory sterilization is wrong because humans possess a yearning to reproduce.

Proscription of free speech is wrong because it violates the natural human urge to express oneself and communicate ideas to others. Confiscation of property is wrong because humans endeavor to produce things that enrich their lives or can be traded for other things that do so. Even if flouting the Natural Law benefits a majority (as is typically the claim), there will always be someone who pays the price of having their human nature transgressed upon.

We acquire political rights by virtue of the government. For example, most of the rights recognized in the Constitution are Natural Rights. However, some rights—such as the right to be indicted by a grand jury before prosecution—depend upon the Constitution rather than the Natural Law for their existence. Is there a fundamental yearning to have government prosecutors present your case to a grand jury, at which no judge or defense counsel is present, and the makeup of which is usually timid souls eager to please the prosecutors? Certainly not. This approach to justice has nothing to do with human inclinations and the Natural Law. Instead, it is a right that we enjoy by virtue of being under the jurisdiction of the federal government as opposed to simply being human. Unlike Natural Rights, political rights rely upon government for their existence; they cannot be considered self-evident.

By what standards should we judge
the validity of the Human Laws
that our government enacts?

B ecause human suffering results when man-made laws conflict with the Natural Law and because the very purpose of Human Law is to enforce Natural Rights, human laws are only valid to the extent that they uphold the Natural Law. St. Thomas Aquinas noted that "[I]f any point in [human law] deflects from the law of nature, it is no longer a law but a perversion of the law." We will, however, most likely obey a law regardless of whether it comports with Natural Law if the consequence of disobeying is punishment. By imposing a requirement of validity, though, we ensure that our government is constrained by the Natural Law. All of us should be constantly questioning the validity of our officials' commands. If those officials violate the Natural Law, then we must do everything in our power to right their wrongs and restore our freedom. At the simplest, it will entail voting them out of office; at the most extreme, it will mean abolishing that government altogether.

The Declaration of Independence and Our Founding Fathers: How Far We've Strayed

What is a Right?

A right is a gift from God that extends from our humanity. Our right to life and our right to develop our personalities; our right to think as we wish, to say what we think, to publish what we believe; our right to worship or not worship; our right to travel, to defend ourselves, to use our own property as we see fit; our right to due process—to fairness—from the government; and our right to be left alone—all these rights stem from our humanity. These are Natural Rights that we are born with. The government doesn't give them to us, the government doesn't pay for them, and the government can't take them away unless a jury finds that we have violated someone else's rights.

What does the American Constitution say about Natural Rights?

The Ninth Amendment states that "[t]he enumeration in the Constitution, of certain rights, shall not be construed to deny or disparage others retained by the people." What would constitute those other "rights retained by the people" if not Natural Rights? Congress and the president cannot take away those rights by enacting a law or issuing a command. Also, just as the Bill of Rights constrains the federal government, the Fourteenth Amendment protects individuals from the states encroaching on our Natural Rights: "No State shall make or enforce any law which shall abridge the privileges or immunities of citizens of the United States." Again, what would be the basis of the privileges or immunities of American citizens if not our Natural Rights?

What did British philosopher John Locke—
the grandfather of the American Revolution—
say about societies, and what commentary on
twenty-first-century US government do his
ideas offer?

Societies form naturally because individuals come together in an attempt to acquire various goods and property, and coming together will inevitably lead to conflict because of man's fallible nature. It is for this reason alone that governments form, with their only role being the protection and preservation of every individual's natural rights—and the only way the government gains this power is through the consent of the individuals involved.

According to Locke, if governments abuse their powers, or if individuals do not consent to their governance, it is the right of the people to revoke their consent or to alter or abolish the government. Now consider the role of government today. Did anyone actually consent to this government? Where and how do you go about giving your consent? Do those in power even ask for our consent, or is it assumed that we implicitly consent, and, more importantly, how do we revoke that implied consent? Basically, it seems that modern American thought has replaced the theory that the only just role of government is to *protect* our natural rights with the theory that the role of government is to *give* us our rights.

What kind of government did Thomas Paine, the author of the 1776 pamphlet Common Sense, propose for the colonies, and how does it compare to today's reality?

Imagine a pyramid of power with the king being on top, then the nobles and military right below him, with the common folk, accounting for most of the population, all the way at the bottom. How could one man be expected to create all the laws that were designed to govern the lives of so many people? Paine attempted to flip this pyramid. The common folk would make the laws that were to govern their own lives and property. They would then elect representatives who would create laws in accordance with the laws of nature (Natural Rights), and these laws would govern social interactions between individuals with the only goal being the preservation of each individual's rights. These representatives would elect a leader to enforce those laws regarding intercolonial matters, all of which were in accordance with the Natural Law.

Today, we have a congress with 500 members who create the laws for approximately 310 million Americans. Clearly, happiness, peace, and liberty cannot be achieved when one institution is making laws for an entire population, especially when the population it is making laws for is 620,000 times larger than the population of the people making the laws.

C onsider our government's role in British Petroleum's
summer 2010 oil-spill disaster in the Gulf of Mexico.

- After the Exxon Valdez spill off of Alaska in 1989
  had been cleaned up and nearly paid for by Exxon,
  the oil companies lobbied Congress for liability
  limits. A Republican Congress and President
  Clinton together made it the law that oil companies would be limited to pay $75 million for clean-
  ups and that the taxpayers—that would be
  you—would pay the rest. In return, the feds would
  be able to tell the oil companies where to drill and
  how to transport their oil.
- British Petroleum (BP) asked the State of
  Louisiana if it could drill in five hundred feet of
  water, and Louisiana said it could.
- The federal government vetoed that decision and
  said BP could only drill in five thousand feet of water.
  Never mind that no oil company had ever cleaned up
  a broken well at that depth and never mind that the
  feds had never monitored a broken well at that depth

and never mind that BP only needed to set aside $75 million in case something went wrong.

- Disaster struck. The feds did nothing. Oil gushed out in an amount that is so great as to be immeasurable. Political pressure grew. President Obama eventually panicked because he believes that his federal government can right every wrong, regulate every activity, and protect us from every catastrophe.
- The president even invoked powers that allow *him to supervise the cleanup using BP personnel and equipment.* And the oil still gushed.
- Then the president stopped all oil drilling in the Gulf, putting thousands out of work.
- Then the president demanded billions from BP so his team could decide who gets it, and a terrified BP gave him all the cash he asked for.

So the government that foolishly limited BP's maximum liability, the government that claimed it knew where best to drill, the government that actually stopped locals from protecting their own shoreline—that would be that same government that bankrupted Social Security, Medicare, Medicaid, the Post Office, Amtrak, and virtually everything it has managed—now wants to decide who gets BP's cash. Our government cannot protect us from every catastrophe, especially ones its rules have facilitated.

Under the Contracts Clause, the states are prohibited from interfering with obligations under private contracts. But the Supreme Court has never faithfully interpreted the clause. In *Home Building & Loan Association v. Blaisdell* (1934), the US Supreme Court held that a Minnesota law prohibiting banks from foreclosing mortgages that were in default did not violate the Contracts Clause.

Despite the majority's approval of this interference with free contracts and undue regulation of commerce, the dissenting justices remained true to the text and spirit of the Constitution, including its prohibition on interference with contracts. In his dissent, Justice Sutherland wrote:

Whether the legislation under review is wise or unwise is a matter with which we have nothing to do. Whether it is likely to work well or work ill presents a question entirely irrelevant to the issue. The only legitimate inquiry we can make is whether it is constitutional. If it is not, its virtues, if it has any, cannot save it; if it is, its faults cannot be invoked to accomplish its destruction. *If the provisions of the Constitution be not upheld when they pinch as well as when they comfort, they may as well be abandoned*"[1] (emphasis added).

Justice Sutherland wrote that the "effect of the Minnesota legislation, though serious enough in itself, is of trivial significance compared with the far more serious and dangerous inroads upon the limitations of the Constitution."

What is significant about the 1934 case *Home Building & Loan Association v. Blaisdell,* when the US Supreme Court allowed Minnesota banks to foreclose mortgages that were in default?

B *laisdell* is extremely significant in that it marks both the clear turning point away from the Court's laissez-faire, free-market philosophy and a repudiation of the Contracts Clause. The Court was no longer concerned about keeping the markets open and free. It was no longer concerned with keeping the government small. It was no longer concerned with enforcing freely consented-to agreements. Its new priority was "the common good" and making sure that the government would provide for it.

Justice Antonin Scalia once cautioned: "If the courts are free to write the Constitution anew, they will, by God, write it the way the majority wants; the appointment and confirmation process will see to that. This, of course, is the end of the Bill of Rights, whose meaning will be committed to the very body it was meant to protect us against: *the majority*" (emphasis added).

Yes, it did. In 1890 the Supreme Court suggested that it would allow a state to interfere with a private contract in violation of the Contracts Clause if the state did so under its police power. Imagine the Supreme Court turning a blind eye to the Constitution and the Contracts Clause just because a state claims it has a "valid police purpose" for interfering with a contract! This principle was later expanded to allow state activities that were nothing more than the redistribution of wealth.

In fact, when the Supreme Court upheld the Minnesota law that prevented mortgage holders from foreclosing on mortgages for a two-year period, it was an unforgivable assault on the Natural Law right to contract. This ruling sanctioned precisely the sort of legislation that the Contracts Clause was written to prevent. What is the value of a binding contract if, when it stings one of the parties, the state comes to the rescue?

In this case, the Court dismissed the Founders' intent for the Contracts Clause as irrelevant. Chief Justice Hughes wrote, "It is no answer . . . to insist that what the provision of the Constitution meant to the vision of that day, it must mean to the vision of our time."

This is the strongest statement of this kind ever made in constitutional history. *The Court explicitly held that the Founders' intent is irrelevant in the interpretation of constitutional language,* and thus the meaning of the fundamental law of the land changes with each generation.

If the reasoning in the previous entry was controlling in all constitutional interpretation, then the Constitution could be interpreted to mean anything that serves present-day convenience. The Court also stressed that the law "was not for the mere advantage of particular individuals but for the protection of a basic interest in society," meaning that it is to serve a greater societal good rather than protect the freedom of the individual from the abuses of government.

Wrong.

The Constitution was intended to protect individuals and minorities from the tyranny of a more numerous and powerful majority.

The dissent of Justice Sutherland has become a mantra for all who believe in limited government: "If the provisions of the Constitution be not upheld when they pinch as well as when they comfort, they may as well be abandoned."

In *Lochner*, the Supreme Court declared unconstitutional a New York State law that limited the number of hours a baker could work. How dare a state in the land of opportunity try to steal the liberty of a laborer to work and a small businessperson to employ him? That is precisely what the New York legislature attempted. But the *Lochner* court, one hundred years ago, would have none of it!

The Court held that the "state had no reasonable ground for interfering with liberty by determining the hours of labor for individuals who are free to work as they choose." It found that the law interfered with freedom of contract, it did not serve a valid police power, and it thus violated the Fourteenth Amendment's Due Process Clause because it took away property (the fruits of the agreement) without a trial.

Firmly, the Court established that the "freedom, or liberty of contract was a basic, fundamental right protected by the liberty and property provisions of the Due Process

Clause of the Fifth and Fourteenth Amendment." As a natural right, freedom of contract received the greatest judicial protection by the Constitution.

From *Lochner* on, the Court continued to protect natural economic liberties, such as freedom of contract, freedom to pursue a livelihood, and freedom to practice a trade or a profession, using the Due Process Clause of the Fourteenth Amendment.

The judiciary's duty is to scrutinize carefully the constitutionality of all legislation to decide if the government that enacted it had the power to do so and to determine if the legislation violates the Natural Law. The *Lochner* court held that legislation is constitutional if it does not interfere with the freedom of contract and it serves a "legitimate police purpose."

The phrase *legitimate police purpose* referred to "those powers that relate to safety, health, morals, and the general welfare of the public." With great foresight, the justices cautioned that laws purporting to be such exercises of "valid police powers" were typically just shielded attempts to redistribute wealth by regulating the labor or the hours of one group at that group's expense or at the expense of another group.

The intrusive, suffocating law struck down in *Lochner* prevented bakery owners and bakers from contracting for as many hours of work as they wished. Thus the law interfered with the bakers' freedom of contract. This paternalism robbed them of "their independence of judgment and of action." What could be worse than a country where the government tells you that you can live your dreams if you work "hard" enough, but does not allow you to work as "hard" as you choose?

These "watching out for you" regulations are not rules in a game. They are restrictions on one's livelihood. When the government is acting like an overprotective parent, it forces dependence upon itself.

Politicians create laws under the guise of "helping people" in order to ensure that they have a dependent group of people to continue to vote for them. One of the cruelest things that one can do is to take perfectly capable people and brainwash them to believe that they are not capable.

We may have abandoned such self-evident truths that the *Lochner* Court reminded us of so eloquently, but it remains one of the most important and frequently cited cases in Supreme Court history. It serves as the yard marker in the ideological battles between the free market Natural Law originalists and the New Deal regulatory state Positivists.

During the *Lochner* era, the Court used the substantive due process doctrine as well as the Commerce Clause as protective shields over freedom's guarantees. Which method the Court employed depended on which government actor was doing the infringing. If a *state* adopted a minimum wage law, it would have been struck down as violating the Due Process Clause of the Fourteenth Amendment. However, if it were the *federal government* that attempted to adopt such a law, it was invalidated as exceeding the power given to Congress by the Commerce Clause.

Both were a means to an end. The Supreme Court zealously promoted capitalism, free enterprise, property rights, and freedom to contract from overreaching government regulations. The justices believed these regulations violated individual natural rights and the Constitution, and were nothing short of paternalistic means to increase government power for the sake of redistributing wealth. And during this period of American history, there occurred the most remarkable industrial revolution—indeed the greatest economic growth—the country had ever seen, unaccompanied by increased taxes and bigger government.

The Tenth Amendment has tragically become almost a nullity at the present point in our history, but this is what it says: "The powers not delegated to the United States by the Constitution, nor prohibited by it to the states, are reserved to the states respectively, or to the people."

Hear the Court's stance, grounded as it is in the Constitution: "Our Federal Government is one of *enumerated powers*" (emphasis added). The Court went on to state in ominous terms, "The control by Congress over interstate commerce cannot authorize the exercise of authority not entrusted to it by the Constitution. The maintenance of authority of the states over matters purely local is as essential to the preservation of our institutions as is the conservation of the supremacy of the federal power in all matters entrusted to the Nation by the Federal Constitution."

Even at a more basic level, we must remember that the Founders envisioned a loose confederation of states. They firmly believed in the idea that states should remain potent in governing themselves. Why were they so adamant about this idea? The answer lies in the fact that they had just escaped the tyranny of a king who thought he knew best how to govern local colonies from across an ocean.

The Founders knew two things in this regard. First, proximity is power. Governments and political leaders are best held accountable to the will of the people when government is local. Second, the people of a state know what is best for them; they do not need bureaucrats, miles away in Washington, DC, governing their lives.

How did we end up with a social welfare state in America, where the feds have unchecked runaway power, the states comparatively little, and Americans have fewer freedoms?

Between the late 1800s and early 1900s, the Court's aggressive advancement of ideals like economic due process and a laissez-faire economy were constructions of the law that were faithful to the Constitution. The Court vigorously enforced "freedom to choose." Sadly, the Court soon retreated from upholding the Constitution and the Natural Law.

In 1937, the Court reversed course and began upholding New Deal legislation, and we've been feeling the effects of that retreat ever since. The modern Supreme Court's expansive reading of the Commerce Clause is but one example of the slippery slope created by Franklin Delano Roosevelt's New Deal. Before the New Deal, the Commerce Clause was interpreted as giving Congress power to regulate interstate commerce and to regulate intrastate matters provided that they substantially affected interstate commerce. Production and the conditions of production were reserved to the states because commerce only meant "the movement of goods." And under the Tenth Amendment, the states did not delegate to the federal government the power to regulate any other aspects of commercial activity.

Under principles espoused in the New Deal cases, the Court officially changed its position, eventually holding that the Commerce Clause allows regulation of production as well as movement of commercial goods,[2] no matter how minute or local.

The New Deal was a collection of regulations and agencies designed to pull us from the depths of the Great Depression, the Constitution notwithstanding. Did FDR understand the Constitution? Did FDR realize the long-term implications for human freedom of his New Deal? Did he care?

The New Deal may have helped some people in the short term, but it codified socialism, evaded the Constitution, disregarded the Natural Law, and put individualism on the path to extinction. No doubt, FDR boldly led us out of the Great Depression and through the Second World War. Unfortunately, he did this in a most unconstitutional manner. And his successors followed his lead.

Due to the country's deep public reverence for the man, by 1937 the Supreme Court feared using the judicial review it had established. Who then would tell Roosevelt that no matter how good his intentions were, they were, emphatically, not being carried out in a constitutional manner?

The Great Depression created pressure to abandon the Constitution's free market underpinnings. In this uniquely desperate time, popular perception was that government regulations would improve the economic state of those suffering, and when people are hungry, they tend not to think about the Constitution, limited government, or the Natural Law.

Legal Positivists gained intellectual prominence and attacked Natural Law principles that uphold freedom of contract and property rights. They argued instead that there were no natural rights to contract or to property and that the Court was simply making political choices that could be altered if the situation necessitated it.

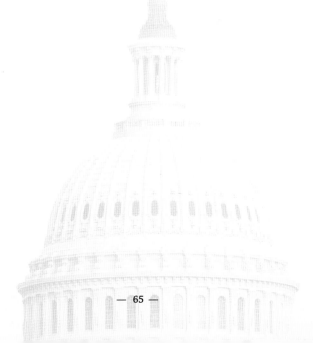

Why doesn't the Court use its power to keep things constitutional?

T he answer lies in the momentum created by FDR's unchallenged New Deal.

After the *Blaisdell* case, the Court effectively gave up trying to uphold the Natural Law right to contract. Its new priority was "the common good" and making sure that the government would provide for it. The Court also distanced itself from its role as a check on Congress and a guard of legislative constitutionality. "Whether the free operation of the normal laws of competition is a wise and wholesome rule for trade and commerce is an economic question that this court need not consider or determine . . . [and one with which] the courts are both incompetent and unauthorized to deal."

That lovely sentiment is from the *Blaisdell* dissent.

I see the Supreme Court beginning to bow to political pressures in 1934 when New York adopted a Milk Control law that established a board empowered to set a minimum retail price for milk.

Nebbia was a store owner who sold milk *below* the minimum price. He sold it cheaper than the State wished. In *Nebbia v. New York* (1934), the Court reversed the premise that government could only regulate to achieve a narrow and valid police purpose so long as it does not interfere with the constitutionally granted rights of freedom of contract and freedom of property.

"The state is free to adopt whatever economic policy may reasonably be deemed to promote public welfare and to enforce that policy by legislation adapted to its purpose." The Court held there was nothing "peculiarly sacrosanct" about milk prices that insulated them from government regulation and upheld the law. What happened to the Contracts Clause? What happened to free enterprise? Is it not good for consumers—the common good—to pay less for milk rather than more?

To ensure that the Court would continue in the vein of *Nebbia* and fall in line with the political demands of the times, Roosevelt and his attorney general concocted a plan that would dramatically alter the course of his presidency, and the nation's history.[3]

The president proposed increasing the number of justices on the Supreme Court and in the federal judiciary. This plan drew intense opposition, even from supporters of the New Deal programs, because it was a threat to the independence of the judiciary and to the Constitution itself. In the midst of congressional, editorial, and public reaction to the "court packing" plan, and perhaps as a result of it, the year 1937 saw cases involving both substantive due process and the scope of the Congress's commerce power that brought about a new era of the federal government's paternalism and a massive expansion of federal government power that saddles and socializes Americans to this day.

Then Justice Owen Roberts switched ideological sides and brought a conclusive end to the Constitution as protector of natural rights, the free market, and federalism, which had characterized the Court's decisions for the preceding 150 years. His decisive vote as part of the five-to-four majority against many minimum wage programs swung the other way to become the five-to-four majority. The court-packing plan was withdrawn.

Clearly, Roosevelt had won the battle to keep the courts from invalidating his legislation by threatening to dilute the ranks of judges and justices who disagreed with his understanding of the Constitution. Imagine the audacity of a president trying to alter the entire federal judiciary in order to intimidate a justice into switching ideological sides? Talk about dirty politics. Talk about utter disregard for the Constitution. Talk about it all you want. It worked.

- *West Coast Hotel v. Parrish* (1937): Elsie Parrish, an employee of the West Coast Hotel Company, still received subminimum wage compensation for her work. Parrish sued to recover the difference between the wages paid to her and the minimum wage fixed by state law.

  In "Constitution speak," that means that the government is free to regulate in the economic realm as long as its purpose is legitimate. The Court opined, "Freedom of contract is a qualified, and not an absolute, right. There is no absolute freedom to do as one wills or to contract as one chooses. The guaranty of liberty does not withdraw from legislative supervision . . . the making of contracts, or deny to government the power to provide restrictive safeguards." Where did this come from? I'll give you a hint: not from the Constitution or its Contracts Clause.

  Congress was now set to become the paternalistic, legislative watchdog, guarding individuals from the "evils" of free market activity. The federal judiciary would now defer to Congress as long as the laws and regulations were "reasonable." But what would constitute "reasonable"? We were headed down the slippery slope to the modern social welfare state.

- *United States v. Carolene Products Co.* (1938): The Court upheld the federal government's Filled Milk Act of 1923, which banned the interstate shipment of "filled milk" (milk with skimmed milk and vegetable oil added). Now the power to regulate ("to make regular") interstate commerce includes the power to ban products not intrinsically harmful, but just distasteful—distasteful in Congress's opinion.

  The Court went even further in this case than it did in *Parrish* and said that economic regulations need only have "any conceivable" rational basis, regardless of Congress's actual intent. That is, *as long as the Court or the government's lawyers defending the statute can drum up any hypothetical congressional intention for passing a law that would serve a rational end, it would pass constitutional muster.* Federal law was now in the imaginations of whatever a member of Congress or federal judge or government lawyer could "conceive" it to be.

- *NLRB v. Jones & Laughlin Steel Corp.* (1937): Congress determined that labor-management disputes were directly related to the flow of interstate commerce and thus could be regulated by the federal government. The steel industry challenged the power of Congress to establish the Board, and the actions taken by it, as well as the constitutionality of the act itself. The Court upheld the Board's actions and the constitutionality of the act and ruled that the National Labor Relations Board may regulate those industrial activities, which had the "*potential* to burden or restrict interstate commerce."

To make matters worse, the same Court that had yet to define the right *to work* as "fundamental," and thus entitled to protection from the judiciary, said the right *to organize a labor union* was "fundamental."

The Court also said the federal government had the right to intervene in labor disputes. The Supreme Court would now allow Congress to pass legislation that would attempt to equalize bargaining power between employers and their employees. "The exploitation of a class of workers who are in an unequal position with respect to bargaining power and are thus relatively defenseless . . . casts a burden for their support upon the community." Doesn't that sound more like Karl Marx than Thomas Jefferson? These judicial about-faces were no doubt a reaction to the disastrous economic circumstances of the time and the court-packing stunt much more so than they were true reflections of what is actually a fundamental right under the Constitution.

When the Supreme Court unanimously affirmed the right of Congress to exercise "to its utmost extent" the powers reserved for it in the Commerce Clause, the Court again upheld the Fair Labor Standards Act.

The most infamous quote goes like this: "The Amendment states but a truism that all is retained that has not been surrendered." The Tenth Amendment would no longer be used by the federal courts to invalidate federal laws in order to protect the zone of power left to the states.

Any congressional regulation would now be regarded as constitutional if that regulation were reasonable (in the minds of the members of Congress who wrote it or the government lawyers who defended it or the federal judges who interpreted it) in order to bring about federal control of any aspect of interstate commerce. Congress would thus have plenary power to establish the terms and circumstances for the interstate shipment of goods (and just about anything else it wants to regulate, control, or stifle).

Justice Stone wrote for the Court that the "motive and purpose of a regulation of interstate commerce are matters for the legislative judgment . . . over which the courts are given *no* control" (emphasis added). The only restriction for such legislative judgment would be the impairment of a fundamental right or liberty, and economic liberties were simply not fundamental.

Between 1937 and 1941, the defenders of the Constitution—dubbed the Four Horsemen—and others left the Supreme Court. Roosevelt ultimately made eight appointments to the Supreme Court, the most of any president except Washington. The Court was now in line with the New Deal's programs and legislation. And it would stay there until 1995.

The Positivist Court's newly embraced deference to the legislature made it possible for the Court to take a number of jurisprudential paths that would have been unheard of during the hands-off approach from 1789 to 1937. A famous example occurred in 1939, when the Court used Congress's newly expanded power under the Commerce Clause to undermine the Second Amendment. In *United States v. Miller* (1939), the Court gave authority to the claim that the Second Amendment merely guarantees a collective right of states to maintain militias and does not guarantee to individuals the right to bear arms.

What did the Rehnquist Court have to say about the Commerce Clause?

The Rehnquist Court observed that there are three categories of permissible regulation under the Commerce Clause. First, Congress may regulate the use of the "channels of interstate commerce," like interstate highways and railroads. Second, it may "regulate and protect" the "instrumentalities of interstate commerce, or persons or things in interstate commerce," like the vehicles in which the goods or persons are physically located when they move across state borders, even if the danger comes from "purely intrastate activities." Third, Congress may regulate activities having a "substantial relation" to interstate commerce. Despite conflicting precedent, the Court concluded that the activity being regulated must "substantially affect" (rather than just "affect") interstate commerce.

Rights and Freedoms That Are Being Violated

THE RIGHT TO OWN PROPERTY

What is the definition of *property*?

The word *property* is not synonymous with land or a house. Your land and your house are types of property. So is your money, and most importantly, your natural rights are your property. And certain rights come with property ownership, like the right to use your property however you see fit; the right to exclude anyone, including the government, from trespassing on your property; and the right to alienate, or transfer, any or all of your property interests. So every time the government limits, restricts, or takes away any of our rights, the government is to provide us with just compensation. When President George W. Bush signed the PATRIOT Act into law, taking away our rights to privacy, due process, *habeas corpus*, free speech, and freedom from illegal searches and seizures, did any of us receive any just compensation for those takings?

Do we really "own" our own property?

Under Alexander the Great, you could never own your own property. Instead, you could only possess property at the same time that you had to both pay to use it and provide your leaders with military service in the event of war. Aren't we currently living under such a system in the US? Individuals are forced to pay income taxes on the fruits of their labor. The product of your labor—wages—becomes your property. But when the government taxes it, the government is basically saying, "We have granted you the right to work. In return you must pay us for the privilege." In addition, we are forced to pay property taxes on our land (if we don't, local authorities seize the land), and the government exercises eminent domain.

The right to private property is fundamental to freedom and individual liberty. However, there are rare instances when it is practical for the government to acquire private property for the general public's use. When the government acquires an individual private property, it is considered a "taking." The source of the government's right to take private property is the "despotic power" or the "eminent domain power."

The traditional uses of the government's eminent domain power include public uses such as building roads, constructing schools, and saving wildlife. Historians have traced this legitimate use of governmental power back to ancient times. The Romans, who constructed straight roads from one end of the empire to the other, used the power of eminent domain to confiscate land on which to build the roads. The aqueducts were erected under similar circumstances. However, the concept of compensating the victims of these confiscations was foreign to the Romans.

A merica's Founding Fathers, even with their strong commitment to private property rights, recognized it was necessary for the government to have some eminent domain power. However, they also correctly recognized that the eminent domain power was subject to much governmental abuse and corruption. Human and economic nature provide the government with an *incentive* to abuse this power.

Left unchecked, the government can simply condemn your property and give it to a favored developer (who contributes to a mayor's or governor's reelection campaign). And the developers do not have to negotiate with you to pay a fair price for your property. Only *you* lose—and how can you complain to the corrupt government that confiscated your land in the first place?

The government's eminent domain power is recognized in the Takings Clause (or the Just Compensation Clause), which is found in the Fifth Amendment to the US Constitution. That clause states, "[N]or shall private property be taken for public use, without just compensation."

This clause is not a positive grant of power to the government. Rather, it places a *limitation* on governmental power, since the Constitution protects the rights of individuals and limits the powers of the government. The Constitution and the Declaration of Independence make clear that the government's only legitimate power is to secure the rights that are guaranteed to the people. As James Madison said, "As a man is said to have a right to his property, he may be equally said to have a property in his rights." Therefore, the Constitution expresses the extremely limited power of the government to condemn private property.

The two pertinent phrases of the Takings Clause are *just compensation* and *public use.* The just compensation requirement ensures that the government fairly compensates the victim of the taking. The victim must be "made whole," meaning that he is economically no worse off as a result of the taking. The government is forbidden from showing up at your door and taking the title to your house, unless it pays you fair market value. It must also pay for your moving expenses, and losses that you incur while establishing yourself elsewhere.

The public use requirement, combined with the just compensation requirement, serves to limit further the government's eminent domain power. This requirement ensures that the taking is legitimate. The government has no right to condemn your property and give it to your neighbor, no matter how much it chooses to compensate you. Accordingly, the government has no authority to take your property—under any circumstances—for a private use.

The Constitution's framers saw firsthand the extent to which a government could abuse private property rights through its eminent domain power. In drafting the Takings Clause, the framers sought to ensure that the US government would not operate as the king of England did.

As the Constitution states, the government may only use its eminent domain power to take private property for a public use. In the eighteenth and nineteenth centuries, the definition of a public use was exactly what it seems to mean: a use by the public. Over the last hundred years, however, corrupt and power-hungry government officials, combined with sympathizing courts, have completely transformed and perverted the Takings Clause.

Tariffs, excise taxes, duties, and sales taxes violate the property rights of the sellers of the goods because the price for their goods is raised, making their business less competitive and less profitable. At the same time, the buyers of these goods are forced to pay higher prices for goods, thus parting with more money than would have been the case had these regulations not been in place.

Why is minimum wage a violation of the US Constitution?

Collective bargaining has increased the economic means of the great majority of working people in the United States by securing decent wages and benefits for union members and driving wages higher even for the unorganized.[1] But business owners are forced to spend more of their money, which is their property, on labor. Paying minimum wage is involuntary: the government forces it upon business owners, thereby violating the Natural Law as well as the Constitution by compelling the owner of a business to negotiate with all of his employees as if they were one. Also, with minimum wage not only requiring higher wages, but prompting higher costs (benefits, pensions, vacation pay) and higher prices as well, the law clearly legislates the government's theft of property from the businessperson.

Why doesn't minimum wage help the people it was intended to help?

Since the poorest members of society also tend to be the least-skilled members, if the minimum wage is set above the level of production that a poor person can achieve with his current skill set, then he will never get a job; and the higher the minimum wage, the higher the barrier poor people have to jump in order to gain employment.

Let me explain: If a person's skill set is valued at $5 an hour by an employer, this valuation will not change just because the government implements an $8 minimum wage. Instead, this person simply will not get the job. What employer will hire a worker who will actually generate a negative return? So, instead of a poor person having the opportunity to hone his skill set and learn the valuable lessons of hard work that would make him more employable, raise his value, grant him a feeling of accomplishment, and increase the wage he can command in the future, this poor person is rendered unemployable and forced to live a substandard life on the welfare dole because of—yes!—government-mandated minimum wages.

Consider, too, how the minimum wage impacts poor teenagers who aren't able to present themselves well in an interview. The main weapon an inner-city teenager would have in this situation would be the willingness to work for a lower wage than his middle-class counterparts would. By giving prospective employers this cost-saving incentive, an inner-city youth could increase his chances of one day successfully competing against the middle- and upper-class teens for employment. Once he gained employment, he could learn useful skills, demonstrate his true value to the employer, learn how a certain business works, build a resume, and command a higher wage in the future. However, since government restricts the ability of an individual to choose how much his own labor is worth, this teenager is forced to remain unemployed, never getting an opportunity to learn very important working skills. This is all, of course, supposedly in the greatest interest of the general welfare of the American people.

R ent control is a government-imposed price ceiling on the amount of money a landlord can charge for rent. In a free market, if the demand for rental apartments is greater than the supply, prices will rise. This rise in prices both reduces the demand and, very importantly, brings forth new supply from investors seeking to take advantage of this new profit opportunity.

When price controls are instituted, however, a shortage results. First, since the price ceiling is set below the market rate for rent, a shortage of low-income apartments naturally follows. The demand for rentals is then spilled over to the noncontrolled sector, which normally consists of higher-priced apartments. This increase of demand, combined with increased fear by landlords to invest in new property since governments could impose rent control on those apartments as well, causes the rental prices of these nonregulated apartments to skyrocket. So, while prices in the controlled sector might be lower, the overall cost of renting will be much higher than the cost a free market would command.

Second, with the increased uncertainty in the whole market, investors will pull their money out and search for greener pastures. This decreased profit incentive discourages landlords from investing in their properties even for such things as ordinary maintenance, thus causing the property to deteriorate over time. No wonder socialist economist Assar Lindbeck said this: "In many cases rent control appears to be the most efficient technique presently known to destroy a city—except for bombing."[2]

The Interstate Commerce Clause in the Constitution was designed to give Congress the power to regulate commerce with foreign nations, states, and Native Americans. The original meaning of the word *regulate* was "to keep regular," and its sole purpose was to prevent states from creating tariffs to be used to the detriment of merchants in other states. When the feds sought to fine Ohio farmer Roscoe Filburn for growing and consuming too much wheat, the Supreme Court of the United States ruled in 1942 that if farmers were allowed to grow any amount of wheat they wished, this freedom would, in the aggregate, affect not only the price of wheat but interstate commerce as well, thus validating for Congress the power to regulate interstate commerce in this instance—despite the fact that everyone knows that growing wheat in your backyard and consuming it is not a commercial activity, that it takes place in one state, and that it has *no* measurable effect on interstate commerce.

Congress has since abused this power to no end. Not only has the government regulated the remedies for defaulting on loans, not only has it regulated the amount of wheat grown in our backyards, but it has also regulated the number of hours per day bakers can spend turning that wheat into bread, the wages they can be paid, and the temperatures of their ovens!

What argument did the government make
about someone's crop of medical marijuana
and Congress's use of the Commerce Clause?

Gonzalez v. Raich (2004) is the case of Angel Raich and Diane Monson, two chronically ill women who suffered debilitating pain, such that their physicians prescribed medical marijuana to relieve pain. The Court wanted to limit the growth of their marijuana.

Writing for the majority, Justice John Paul Stevens wrote, "When Congress decides that the 'total incidence' of a practice poses a threat to a national market, it may regulate the entire class." Last time I checked, Justice Stevens, there was no "legal" national market for marijuana!

The Court also had this to say: "Congress had a rational basis for concluding that leaving home-consumed marijuana outside federal control would similarly affect price and market conditions." Now, just where is the local marijuana store? What are the prevailing, congressionally regulable prices and market conditioners?

Justice Clarence Thomas wrote an eloquent dissent, which in one paragraph blew away the majority's position:

Diane Monson and Angel Raich use marijuana that has never been bought or sold, that has never crossed state lines, and that has had no demonstrable effect on the national market for marijuana. If Congress can regulate this under the Commerce Clause, then it can regulate virtually anything—and the Federal Government is no longer one of limited and enumerated powers. . . . By holding that Congress may regulate activity that is neither interstate nor commerce under the Commerce Clause, the Court abandons any attempt to enforce the Constitution's limits on federal power.[3]

The Community Reinvestment Act (CRA) of 1977 was one of the many ways the government attempted to provide affordable housing to low-income people. The CRA essentially mandates that banks contract with less-than-desirable borrowers in an effort to increase home ownership across the nation. During the Carter administration, people accused mortgage lenders of racism because poor urban dwellers—who were mostly black—were being denied loans, while suburban whites were not. Seeking to reduce "discriminatory" credit practices against low-income people, Congress got involved in order to get more money into the hands of minorities to increase home ownership. (This is not the job of the government, by the way.)

The CRA made it legal for the government to twist the arms of private banks to make loans to less-than-creditworthy borrowers, thereby forcing private banks to associate with clients not of their choosing, but rather of the government's choosing. To hold control over these lenders, Congress empowered a number of regulatory agencies to punish those banks that were not meeting the credit needs of "low-income, minority, and distressed neighborhoods." Bullied into loosening their standards, banks made questionable loans to those who could not afford them.

Generally, banks make loans based on the personal variables of the borrowers, such as the size of the mortgage payment relative to income, credit history, and income verification. But in the wake of the Community Reinvestment Act, the federal government informed banks that participation in "credit-counseling" programs was sufficient as proof of a low-income applicant's ability to make mortgage payments: "Banks and lenders, forget about those other silly factors. You know, factors like *the numbers*. Trust us. We are the government." Loans were being handed out by private banks—because the government mandated it—like candy on Halloween. As Michael Lewis reported in *The Big Short*, a Mexican strawberry picker with an annual income of $14,000 was given a loan for a $700,000 home. In what kind of world is this loan reasonable?

What impact has the government's
Community Reinvestment Act of 1977
had on the US even today?

Interestingly enough, after the government's CRA scheme caused the real estate bubble that burst in September 2008, the solution the government proposed was to prop up housing prices to extreme heights that were artificially bid up by speculators. In other words, the program designed to provide more affordable housing kicked many homeowners out of their houses and wrecked the economy. The government then attempted to solve the wreckage by keeping housing prices higher or at more unaffordable levels for poor people. The irony of government actions never ceases to amaze me.

Furthermore, in passing the Community Reinvestment Act of 1977, the government ignored a crucial little fact: businesses have the right to contract *freely* with individuals or companies with whom they *freely* choose to contract. That is their fundamental right.

THE FREEDOM OF SPEECH

What was the intent of the Founding Fathers
as they considered freedom of speech?

The First Amendment line "Congress shall make no law . . . abridging the freedom of speech" recognizes the natural right to free expression and restrains Congress from interfering with that right. Furthermore, the freedom to speak, unlike the freedom to swing one's arms or shoot a gun, will be by its very nature almost never able to harm another. Thus the possibility of one person's speech violating another person's natural rights—and therefore be eligible for government regulation—is extraordinarily slight.

Interestingly, because the Founders believed free speech to be a natural right, they were not always in agreement as to whether it should be inserted into the Constitution. Since there was no *explicit* grant of power to curtail a right, then there would be no need to recognize that right in the document. After all, an enumeration of rights could prove extraordinarily dangerous, since the inclusion of only some rights could lead people to believe that other rights do not exist.

In what ways is the freedom of speech in accord with the political theory of good governance?

First, freedom of speech is necessary to foster a market-place of ideas. Truth is identified as ideas are exchanged, debated, and nurtured. Only this process, over the course of time, will provide the opportunity for people to recognize truth.

Second, freedom of speech is necessary to an effective government because voters must have access to information in order to make well-informed decisions.

Finally, freedom of speech is at the core of our individuality. As Justice Thurgood Marshall once said, "The First Amendment serves not only the needs of the polity but also those of the human spirit—a spirit that demands self-expression."

Did Americans experience an infringement on our basic right to free speech in the twentieth century?

A setback to our First Amendment right to free speech came in 1917 after the United States entered World War I. Labeling it "the war to end all wars," President Wilson proposed—and Congress enacted—the Espionage Act of 1917.

Under the Espionage Act, roughly two thousand Americans were prosecuted for opposing America's involvement in World War I.[4] Among these prosecutions was the case of Charles T. Schenck, who at the time was an official in the US Socialist Party. Schenck was prosecuted and convicted for conspiring to violate Section 3 of the Act when he supervised the distribution of leaflets likening the draft to slavery and calling involuntary conscription a crime against humanity. Moreover, Schenck urged those subject to the draft not to "submit to intimidation" and to exercise their right to oppose it. Schenck was merely exercising his personal sovereignty over the government: the government is the servant of the people, so the people should be free to discuss with others what actions the servant should take. What right does the servant have to punish his master for giving him certain orders?

- In 1999, a federal jury in Oregon punished the authors of a Web site with a $100 million fine for their provocative antiabortion writings.
- The year before, the United States Supreme Court let stand a federal judge's bizarre perpetual gag order forbidding former jurors from speaking to the media, ever, about their deliberations, absent special permission from the judge herself.
- A Greenville, Mississippi, newspaper reporter was arrested and incarcerated for criminal contempt for publishing a criminal defendant's juvenile record even though it was read aloud in an open courtroom during sentencing.
- In 1997, a Wilmington, North Carolina, newspaper was fined more than $500,000 for publishing truthful details of a secret settlement agreement in an environmental pollution case, although the reporter received the information directly from the court clerk.
- The federal judge handling the Oklahoma City bombing case enforced a gag order forbidding federal prosecutors from communicating with state prosecutors for months beyond the conclusion of the trial.

- And in a first for pop music, in the traditional civil liberties stronghold of Northern California, an up-and-coming rap music artist was arrested and jailed for mouthing angry political lyrics that were unkind to the traditional target of youth-oriented music: the police.

In an unbroken string of First Amendment rulings in the past four decades, the United States Supreme Court has declared that expressive liberties may not be interfered with by the government absent a very strong governmental justification—such as protecting a real and present threat to national security—for doing so.

Whether it is the right of Amish parents to promote their religion by educating young adults at home rather than in high school, or the right of the press to publish the name of a juvenile offender or a rape victim when the press has lawfully obtained the information, the Court has steadfastly protected our First Amendment rights by placing a heavy onus on the government to justify the desired intrusion on the content of individual expressive liberties.

Yet recent cases demonstrate a waning commitment by our courts to act as the protectors of speech liberties guaranteed by the First Amendment. Why is the fundamental right to free speech overlooked when a parole officer decides to have a rap artist arrested because the officer disapproves of what the singer is saying? Where is the strong protection owed to the press when blameless news reporters are arrested and fined for publishing the truth merely because a judge objects? Can the government override the fundamental right to free speech when a judge denies jurors the right to speak about their experiences, cuts off the media's access to jurors willing to speak, or forbids communication among prosecutors long after the judge's control over the participants in the court system has terminated?

Government legislation that defines what is or isn't appropriate speech, what is or isn't incendiary, insinuates that people cannot think for themselves. Such a doctrine is hopelessly subjective and thus offers arbitrary protection of our natural rights. How can judges determine what is of artistic, literary, political, or scientific value? Not even experts in art, literature, politics, and science are able to do so!

Furthermore, it is clearly in violation of the Natural Law to judge speech according to community standards. The Natural Law transcends temporal local cultures.

Finally, the Constitution does not grant the government the power to restrict an individual's speech based on moral or value judgments, nor does the Constitution grant the government the power to criminalize speech. The whole purpose of the First Amendment is to assure that individuals—and not the government—choose what to think, say, publish, hear, or observe. Clearly, however, the government does not view the First Amendment as permitting speech it fears, hates, or finds offensive.

THE FREEDOM OF ASSOCIATION

What does the First Amendment say about the freedom to assemble? In what ways does that freedom play out in real life?

The First Amendment of the US Constitution states that we may voluntarily gather, come together, or assemble ourselves in whatever peaceful associations we choose, and the government cannot interfere with those choices. Note that this fundamental right is worded such that it restricts government action; it does not restrict our action.

However, just because the Constitution says that we *can* associate with any individual we please does not mean that we *may* associate with any individual we please. The freedom to associate is predicated on the existence of mutual consent: each person must agree to associate with the other person. For example, when A and B agree to associate with each other, both A and B have that freedom. But if A wants to associate with B and B does not wish to associate with A but is *required* to do so, then B is not legally free to reject that association with A. Rather, B is being *forced* to associate with A. This concept, called forced association, is completely counter to our natural rights as free individuals because it infringes upon our right of free choice: it is counter to the Constitution.

As a result, the right to associate has two components. First, we are free to associate with those who accept us. This is called positive freedom of association. Second, we are free to abstain from associations of which we do not approve. This is called negative freedom of association. Both aspects are integral to the freedom of association as a whole, both are natural rights, and both are protected by the First Amendment.

What if someone exercises the right not to associate and is accused of discrimination?

Let me begin with a story. Jennifer Portnick, a 5-foot-8-inch, 240-pound woman, applied to become an aerobics instructor at Jazzercise, a private gym that markets itself as "the world's leading dance-fitness program." When Jazzercise chose not to hire her, citing its company policy that instructors must have a "fit appearance," Ms. Portnick took her case to the San Francisco Human Rights Commission.[5] After all, the law forbids employers from discriminating on the basis of a person's height or weight. The Commission ruled in favor of Ms. Portnick and *forced* the gym to hire this 5-foot-8-inch, 240-pound woman as its newest aerobics instructor.[6]

The state is grossly overstepping its authority here! The government does not own Jazzercise. The state does not have the right to tell Jazzercise who it can and cannot hire. The government does not have the right to intrude on a private business owner's right to run his business as he pleases. The government does not have the right to dictate to Jazzercise what is and what is *not* good business practice. All these decisions are *solely* the interests of the business owner and his or her team of advisors.

This ridiculous illustration aptly demonstrates how the government, without restraint, continues to violate the fundamental rights of free individuals and private business. In the case of Jazzercise, the state completely obliterated a private business's fundamental freedom of association. After all, the freedom to associate means freedom *not* to associate.

Do we have the right to discriminate?

Even when it is defined in terms of our freedom to associate, the concept of discrimination is difficult to accept today because we hear the word *discrimination* and think of racial discrimination. Our society teaches us that racial discrimination is wrong, and I completely agree. Racism is morally wrong and thus deplorable. But when the government tells a private business owner whom he or she can associate with on his or her own property, a constitutional and legal problem arises. It is not the government's job to insert itself in this manner. It is the government's job to protect the voice and actions of the unpopular opinion. While the racist may be in the minority this time, the pacifist, agriculturalist, Jew, or Scientologist may be in the minority next time. It may feel like the world is upside down when we are defending the racist, misogynist, or the homophobe, but the Rule of Law is in place to protect the minority from the tyranny of the majority.

I n a word, yes. As we have seen, because we have the right to associate, we also have the right to discriminate. As a result of these regulations, free individuals are required to associate with *everyone*. Again, we call this forced association, and forced association is unnatural and unconstitutional.

In addition to violating our rights in its quest to eliminate discrimination, the government is wholly inconsistent in its efforts. The government only mandates that we associate with everyone in theory, but the state makes exceptions to these antidiscrimination laws all the time.

Take professional sports, for example. Why isn't the government forcing the National Football League (NFL), Major League Baseball (MLB), or the National Basketball Association (NBA) to add women to their all-male rosters? If these private teams and organizations have the right to discriminate against women and to associate with men only, should not other corporations and groups be allowed the same liberty, to associate with whom they please?

The NFL, MLB, and NBA must have the right to discriminate against women because they are private entities.

That is their First Amendment-protected right. Private businesses have that freedom, and the government must not interfere. But the government must also be consistent in its noninterference.

In Alabama, it used to be a crime for blacks and whites to play cards at the same table or walk down the same sidewalks. In privately owned factories, blacks and whites were required to look out different windows. As witnesses in court, blacks and whites had to swear on different Bibles. Black barbers could not give white people haircuts. Blacks and whites had to check out books in separate library branches. This system of legalized segregation was fully in place by 1910 in every state in the South.

In the passage of these dreadful Jim Crow laws, the government singlehandedly stripped blacks and whites of the freedom to associate with whom they pleased. Take note: Jim Crow laws were written, implemented, and enforced by the government. They were not the result of free individual action. Jim Crow legislation was interfering with the right of individuals to run their businesses as they see fit! It is simple economics and wise business practice to integrate.

The Civil Rights Act of 1964 prohibits both the state and the federal government from making decisions based on race. Two provisions of the act violate the fundamental rights of individuals, specifically, the freedom of association and basic property rights. The government does not have the authority to tell an individual how to run his business (for instance, whom he allows in, whom he sells to, or how he manages his finances). We may not agree with this business owner, but the government must defend the individual's right to run his business the way he chooses. It is his property and his business.[7]

What is the National Labor Relations Act (NLRA) and who benefits from it?

In the wake of the severe economic troubles during the Great Depression, Congress passed the National Labor Relations Act (NLRA). First, the NLRA requires private employers to work with certified unions (certified not by a neutral third party, but by the government), thereby limiting the means by which private employers work and relate with their very own employees. Through the NLRA, the government demolishes the owner's right of association.

Second—and ironically—the NLRA also violates the associational freedoms of the very people it seeks to protect: the individual workers. Their rights are violated in two ways. First, when the majority of the workers at a company has approved a union as the "bargaining agent," that union becomes the sole bargaining agent for all workers. It is the voice both of those who voted for the union and those who voted against the union. As a result, individual workers are barred from even representing themselves; they have been forced to associate with the majority. Furthermore, the NLRA compels workers to pay union dues whether or not they voted for the union in the first place. The concept is called "union security," but it is simply forced association.[8]

There is *one party* that benefits from this forceful, freedom-negating federal regulation: the government. As a result of this labor union-private employer arrangement, the state grows in power, asserting a substantial amount of authority over the private sphere.

Professor Charles Baird poses a solution to what he sees as the government's obsession with coercion and its tendency to violate the freedom of association: "If Congress insists on giving unions special privileges of coercion, it should be honest and promulgate a constitutional amendment that says freedom of association does not apply in labor markets. Don't hold your breath."[9]

THE FREEDOM TO TRAVEL

Why is the freedom to travel essential to our democracy?

B asically, the government could eviscerate our constitutional rights simply by limiting the travel of those whose ideas it hates or fears. If we are ever to be free, we must possess an absolute, uninhibited right to travel the world free from interference by government.

Restrictions on one's right to travel connote that the government is the individual's master rather than his servant. If the government usurps this ultimate right from property owners or grants itself a monopoly over certain modes of travel, then clearly the rights of individuals extend only so far as the government wills them. Freedom subject to the government's whim is no freedom at all. Furthermore, circumventing the right to travel is particularly antithetical to the Natural Law and the principle that the temporal is always subject to the immutable.

M ovement is essential to the very existence and recognition of other inalienable rights. If, for instance, you are prevented from leaving your home, your speech is automatically repressed. If you are not permitted to travel, you are kept from practicing your religion with a community of believers. As a result, you are restricted from selecting whom you meet and whom you marry. If your freedom to travel is limited, you are held back from potential employment opportunities and prevented from receiving the education you desire. Clearly, our right to move and be present is inextricably linked to a host of other fundamental rights that we possess as free individuals. Liberty, at its core, is encompassed in the right to leave the place of repression.

What is an example of the
government restricting the physical
travel of American citizens?

On September 12, 1986, during the height of rush hour, New Jersey law enforcement officials set up a police roadblock on the George Washington Bridge that connects New York City to Fort Lee, New Jersey. The stated purpose of the roadblock was to detect persons transporting drugs or under the influence of drugs or alcohol. The roadblock caused massive delays and traffic stalls, causing over one million motor vehicles to come to a complete stop. That is more than one in three hundred Americans—and in some cases drivers waited in excess of four hours.

Most infuriatingly, a woman was forced to give birth on the shoulder of the West Side Highway in New York City, without the benefits of advanced medicine that a hospital would provide. People were prevented from returning home, from attending work, and from seeking proper medical treatment, all so the police could identify individuals carrying drugs. If we as Americans possess an unconditional right to travel freely, how are these government actions allowed to take place?

Financial restrictions typically come in the form of government monopolization of the means of travel. Consider, for instance, the government-subsidized railroad system. This behemoth transportation matrix has survived solely on subsidies, grants, and loans totaling over $25 billion throughout its existence. Despite these handouts, the prices of train tickets have continued to grow over the years. As I write this chapter, the *cheapest* round-trip ticket from New York Penn Station to Washington, DC, Union Station is $144. A round-trip airline ticket on JetBlue from New York to DC came to $139. Yes, it is cheaper and thus more cost-efficient to travel on a privately owned airline than on a land-based railroad owned and operated by the government. Until the government either has legitimate competition or abdicates control over transportation altogether, these escalating ticket prices will continue to restrict your natural right to move and travel.

In recent years, the most egregious violation of the right to travel is the government's controlled immigration policy. Immigration limitations fundamentally inhibit a person's free will to come and go as he or she pleases. Because the right to move is a natural right, it is not limited to just American citizens. Rather, the right to move is absolutely fundamental: it is possessed by *all* human beings—whether or not they are immigrants. Based on fundamental principles of property, private landowners have the right either to prevent or allow "immigrants" (or anyone) from coming onto their land, but the government does not enjoy a similar right. To suggest otherwise is to say that the government itself somehow "owns" our country and possesses property rights to it.

So upon what legal basis does the government ownership of property rest? It can have no legal basis whatsoever. The government can only vest property rights in itself by providing just compensation to the owner. Any argument that the government has the property right to exclude rests in turn upon the socialistic claim of collective ownership. Therefore, if the state wants a solution to the unlawful stream of immigrants in and out of the country, then it can simply abide by the Natural Law and let them enter legally.

An absolute, uninhibited freedom to travel would *not* have the devastating impact on American jobs that is so often conjectured as long as this freedom is accompanied by the abolition of the minimum wage. When the minimum wage rises, "some jobs that were worth hiring someone to do are no longer worth filling."[10] As a result, there are fewer low-skilled jobs available for people who live here legally. Thus, when the minimum wage rises, employers—in order to cut their costs—hire illegal immigrants at a lower price instead of hiring people who live here legally and paying them the minimum wage.

Alternatively, if the minimum wage were eliminated, employers would pay people who live here legally fair market value rather than the government-mandated amount for the work they do. As a result, immigrants would be less inclined to move here for fear of not finding work.

Opponents of open borders argue that illegal immigrants steal jobs and Social Security numbers, drive down wages by working under the table, and do not pay taxes to the detriment of the nation's budget. But if these men and women were made legal, then they would not have to "steal" jobs and Social Security numbers, but rather they would have their own. They would not drive down wages by working under the table, but rather would work on the books. They would not avoid taxes, but rather would pay them. The net effect of the legalization of immigration would be positive. Immigrants "would gain more of a stake in participating in and preserving our way of life."[11]

THE RIGHT TO PRIVACY

Why does the US Constitution not expressly defend a right to privacy?

I n the eighteenth century *privacy* referred to the bathroom or outhouse. Rather, the Founders used the term *security*, which meant to them essentially the same thing as our contemporary understanding of privacy. For example, the Fourth Amendment states, "The right of the people to be *secure* in their persons, houses, papers, and effects, against unreasonable searches and seizures, shall not be violated, and no warrants shall issue, but upon probable cause" (emphasis added).

Privacy relates to the right or the ability of individuals to determine how much and what information about themselves is to be revealed to others. Additionally, privacy relates to the idea of autonomy, the freedom of individuals to perform or not perform certain acts or to subject themselves to certain experiences.[12]

Now consider the issue of privacy from a different angle. Nowhere in the Constitution is the government granted the power to monitor or regulate our daily conduct. Remember, the Constitution grants power to the federal government and retains for the states and people that power which is not specifically granted. The Constitution keeps the government off our backs. (Well, it is intended to do that.) We retain all unalienable rights, and the right of privacy—"the right to be left alone," as Justice Louis Brandeis wrote in an 1890 law review and later in 1928 when, sitting on the Supreme Court, he addressed the growing trend in technological advances, namely wiretapping, is certainly one of them. So far that hasn't stopped infringements, including the government's proposed use of drones—some the size of golf balls—to watch and listen to us. But the fact remains: by simply being human, you have a right to privacy existing far before the founding of the United States.

In response to the September 11, 2001, terrorist attacks, the New York Police Department (NYPD) implemented the Lower Manhattan Security Initiative (LMSI). Starting in 2007 (if it was so imperative, why did they wait six years?), the NYPD installed over three thousand public cameras and one hundred license-plate reading devices. These publicly-owned cameras, cameras of private landowners, and the publicly-owned license-plate reading devices are fed into an operations center manned by uniformed police. But it is impossible for the police to monitor these thousands of cameras in real time and thereby thwart crime. The best they can hope is to do is review a tape after a crime has occurred and maybe get a lead on a suspect. That is not prevention or safety.

In 1998 the Supreme Court heard the case of *Pennsylvania Board of Probation and Parole v. Scott.* Keith Scott's parole officer believed that Scott had violated a condition of his parole that he not own or possess any weapons. Parole officers arrested Scott, whereupon he surrendered his house keys. The parole officers drove to Scott's residence, where he lived with his parents, and awaited the arrival of Scott's mother. When she arrived, she refused to consent to a search, so they informed her that they were going to search Scott's bedroom without a warrant and without her consent. The parole officers found no evidence of a parole violation in Scott's room, and so they decided to search the rest of the house. In his mother's house they found five unloaded firearms—which were lawfully owned by Scott's stepfather and were unknown to Scott—and proceeded to recommit Scott to jail to serve three years of back time.

The parole officers conducted an illegal search: they entered Scott's mother's home without consent and without obtaining a warrant. In conducting this search, Scott's and his mother's Fourth Amendment rights were violated.

According to the famous exclusionary rule of *Mapp v. Ohio*, the evidence gathered against Scott during the illegal search is considered "fruit of the poisonous tree" and cannot be used against him in court.

The Supreme Court decided that the Fourth Amendment didn't protect Scott, ruling that the exclusionary rule isn't a constitutional guarantee. Essentially, the Court ruled that law enforcement may introduce illegally gathered evidence when the Court says it can.

The five-to-four majority determined that the costs of applying the exclusionary rule exceeded the benefits, in terms of parole violations. Since when is the Supreme Court able to boil the Constitution down to a cost-benefit analysis? As Justice Souter noted in dissent, the Fourth Amendment becomes irrelevant if the police face no consequences, like the exclusion of the evidence they obtain, when they illegally gather evidence. This is yet another instance of the Supreme Court allowing law enforcement an unprecedented amount of power to violate the Constitution.

USA PATRIOT is an acronym for "Uniting and Strengthening America by Providing Appropriate Tools Required to Intercept and Obstruct Terrorism." The PATRIOT Act and its progeny are the most abominable, unconstitutional governmental assaults on personal freedom since the Alien and Sedition Acts of 1798. In effect, the government says, "Give us your freedoms, and we will protect you."

But now federal agents and local police can write their own search warrants, serve them on American financial institutions without the intervention of a judge, and obtain information about *you* without you even knowing it. Even though the USA PATRIOT Act may help law enforcement personnel combat terrorism, it is doing so in a way that is giving more power to the federal government at the expense of the constitutionally guaranteed liberties of every person in America.

Because of such intrusions, we fought the Revolution, we won the Revolution, and we wrote a Constitution. Among other things, we prohibited in that Constitution self-written search warrants. A self-written search warrant? They could write it on the back of a matchbook. Why make them write anything if they can write themselves permission to come into your house? Just let the government ransack the place! That is what the PATRIOT Act has made possible.

A brief aside: In a famous Supreme Court dissent, Justice Louis Brandeis foresaw the articulation by a later generation of justices of the right to privacy. "The makers of our Constitution," he wrote, ". . . conferred, as against the government, the right to be let alone—the most comprehensive of rights and the right most valued by civilized men."[13]

Can federal agents write their own search warrants?

The Fourth Amendment requires that a judge find probable cause of a crime before only she or he can issue a search warrant. Section 505 of the PATRIOT Act unconstitutionally grants federal agents the authority to bypass the Fourth Amendment and write their own search warrants: they can give themselves the authority to search for and seize whatever they wish from among the Act's targets, typically, financial institutions. The Act calls such self-written search warrants "National Security Letters."

Because of Section 505, government officials legally collected and analyzed data on over one million people in Las Vegas during the 2003 Christmas season. But did this massive download of personal data prevent a terrorist attack or an attempted terrorist attack in Las Vegas? No. The government's intelligence was wrong, but its appetite for knowledge of your personal behavior was voracious. You probably did not realize the government has legal authority to track an individual's every move. It does, and this legal authority continuously expands in the effort to fight the War on Terror.

It seems like a well-kept secret because Section 505 grants even further outrageous powers to government agents. Section 505 is, to use the term loosely, limited to personal records from financial institutions, yet *financial institutions* is broadly interpreted. The ridiculous list of financial institutions includes pawnbrokers; travel agencies; car, airplane, and boat dealerships; casinos; medical records; supermarket records; legal records; computer keystrokes; and even the post office. When did sending a letter to Grandma become the financial equivalent of dealing with a broker registered with the Securities and Exchange Commission? The government's designation of different institutions as "financial" is now so vast that federal agents can easily intrude on our daily rituals.

The Act also mandates that the evidence obtained from these wildly unconstitutional, self-authorized search warrants is "constitutionally competent" in criminal prosecutions.[14] In other words, until this section of the Act is challenged, the evidence obtained by these self-issued search warrants is currently legal under federal law, but that evidence is unconstitutional at the same time because it violates the Fourth Amendment. It is bizarre, indeed, for a thing to be both legal and unconstitutional.

The courts continually give law enforcement a free pass to engage in unlawful practices.

One example is the landmark 1952 US Supreme Court case of *Frisbie v. Collins*. It established the principle that a court has the power to put a defendant on trial even if law enforcement broke the law in bringing the defendant into the Court's jurisdiction, as they did with Collins.

It sounds inconceivable, but the Supreme Court authorized the police to *break* the law, including abduction and kidnapping, in order to *enforce* the law. But kidnapping is a federal crime, and the Anti-Kidnapping Act makes it illegal when an individual is "unlawfully seized, confined . . . kidnapped, abducted, or carried away by any means whatsoever" across interstate lines. The federal kidnapping crime applies to both ordinary citizens and officers of the law: *no exception* is made in the statute for either state or federal law enforcement officers.

Thus, the Supreme Court improperly allowed the police to put themselves above the law. When law enforcement uses force and violence illegally to bring a defendant into the courtroom, it is the Court's duty to hold the police accountable for violating the defendant's constitutional rights.

In the criminal justice system, sometimes a "guilty" defendant walks free because the police illegally violated his constitutional rights. While this is unfortunate, the entire system would fall apart if courts failed in their responsibility to ensure that law enforcement does not place itself above the law. The police need a disincentive to keep them from breaking one law in order to enforce another.

Have Americans passively accepted
the president's decree regarding
airport screening procedures?

From my perspective, far more ominous than the rise of big government is the president ruling by decree—and the people's general acceptance of it. The Obama administration's decision to purchase back scanner X-ray machines to use at airports is a prime example. These devices—which *cannot* detect small amounts of plastic explosives on the skin or anything, plastic or metal, hidden in a body cavity—are intended to give the false impression of enhancing public safety.

In order to induce the public into a sheeplike acceptance of these porn scanners, the government offered an alternative even more invasive, unconstitutional, and odious: a public zipper-opening, blouse-removing, testicle-squeezing, breast-pinching alternative. Never mind that you own your own body. Never mind that the Fourth Amendment to the Constitution guarantees that the government cannot touch you against your will without probable cause of crime or a warrant from a judge based on probable cause.

One more point. Congress did not authorize either the porn or the grope alternative. (Indeed, no member of

Congress could vote for this and survive politically!) And the person who will rule by decree—that would be the president—claims he did not authorize this either, but that the "security professionals" who work for him did so. He is fooling no one. He can stop this with a telephone call, but he prefers us to be compliant.

With the passage of Obamacare, your once-private communication with your doctor and medical decisions will now be regulated and monitored by the government. The law requires the Department of Health and Human Services to issue forty thousand laptops, one to each primary care physician in the US, and it requires the physicians to record—for federal bureaucrats to see—whatever you tell your physician and whatever your physician tells you. How can the Supreme Court one day declare a "zone of privacy" that includes the right "to care for one's health and person" and the next day Speaker of the House Nancy Pelosi claim that Congress's power to regulate health care is "essentially unlimited"?

And the invasion of your natural right to privacy does not end there. Now, on an ongoing basis, you will be required to provide personal medical details to an insurance company. What information is more personal than your health? The American Civil Liberties Union describes medical information as "arguably the most personal and private source of data about us," yet the ACLU refuses to challenge Obamacare because of its support for the welfare state.

That means it is up to you to elect officials willing to repeal Obamacare, the PATRIOT Act, the spy cameras, and numerous other pieces of legislation that strip you of your natural right to privacy. Do not ease up in your efforts to fight this political rhetoric, for we never want—as Ben Franklin put it—to lose our essential liberties for temporary safety.

For centuries, governments never interfered with marriages. Instead, marriages were based on religion, parental choice, culture, tradition, and the mutual love of two persons. It certainly is not the government's role to meddle in these most personal of affairs. If the decision-making process that leads to the free choice to marry another person is not considered private, then what can be?

At first, the laws governing marriage were not so restrictive. In the early years, for example, the colonial governments required colonists to register formally their marriages, but it soon became common practice to accept cohabitation as a form of registration. Yet, by the late nineteenth century, state governments began to nullify common-law marriages and exert more control over who could marry whom.[15]

Decades ago the Supreme Court formally settled the issue of interracial marriages, but the nation is currently engulfed in the battle over same-sex marriages. What effect do same-sex marriages have on other individuals? As Jefferson might have said, they neither pick your pocket nor break your leg. They do not harm anyone or violate your natural rights.

YOU OWN YOUR OWN BODY

Does the government interfere with our ownership of our own bodies?

E vidence clearly points to the fact that the government believes it has the right to interfere with your free choices and to monitor what you eat, what you drink, who you sleep with, whether you can donate an organ, and whether you can take that experimental drug from Canada. The government believes that it knows your body better than you do and that it can take better care of your body than you can.

The moment the government interferes with our right to do with our bodies as we please, the state has unconstitutionally, immorally, and unnaturally overstepped its enumerated powers and has violated our rights as individuals. The purpose of the federal government is to protect our constitutional and natural rights, not to restrict or inhibit them.

The federal government thinks it knows what is best for you, your body, and your exchanges. The state claims it has outlawed the sale of organs and body parts for your well-being and safety. Yet by preventing the buying and selling of organs, the government is making it extremely difficult to find sufficient organ donors because there are zero incentives to donate. According to the 1984 federal National Organ Transplant Act, you cannot compensate a person who selflessly donates a kidney (even though the donor has rescued you from fatiguing dialysis and premature death). In fact, this altruistic human being (and violator of the 1984 Act) could be slapped with a $50,000 fine and a felony prison term of up to five years![16] Organ donation is just one more way the government usurps control of decisions—personal and bodily—that are rightfully ours as sovereign individuals.

While some people may be repulsed by the discussion of organ trading for compensation, they shouldn't be, because we already engage in some forms of it. Every day heart valves are replaced, and amputees receive other people's limbs. People exchange their semen, eggs, and plasma for money. For tens of thousands of dollars, women generously rent out their wombs to those who cannot bear children. We donate blood in exchange for little perks like movie tickets and cookies. How can an exchange take place in these situations but not in circumstances involving vital organs? The federal government arbitrarily makes these rules.

Drug prohibition is a failed public policy that must be abolished in the United States. Drugs continue to be available—whether you are looking for them or not—on street corners and in schools across America. Drugs and their dealers flourish just fine under the "watchful" eye of the United States government.

Early in the twentieth century, a number of business tycoons—the DuPonts, Andrew Mellon, and William Randolph Hearst—saw the hemp industry as a major competitor (hemp was an alternative to wood in paper production, for example) and thus a barrier to growth. So they initiated a smear campaign against marijuana, portraying it as a great social evil. In 1937 the Marijuana Tax Law made marijuana illegal. So this mainstay of the American criminal law was based on nothing more than a secretive attempt to destroy business competitors.

Since President Nixon's declaration of the War on Drugs in 1970, the government has spent over $1 trillion trying to combat them. Law enforcement agencies have locked up over 2.3 million people, a higher incarceration rate than any other country.[17] What's more, 60 percent of these incarcerations are for nonviolent crimes. What's the point? These people are not invading my body or my rights or my property—or yours. These people are not harming anyone but themselves, and they have the freedom to do that.

What's more, the state is spending vast amounts of our nation's resources (tax dollars) attempting to fight an unwinnable fight. When something like drugs (or prostitution) is prohibited, black markets pop up with all the corollary problems that surround them. When free exchange is permitted, a legitimate and workable market develops with supply and demand to act as a check.

THE RIGHT TO SELF-DEFENSE

What is the right to bear arms and what does it mean?

The right to possess arms is a fundamental human right. This right is *guaranteed* in the Second Amendment, which states that "[a] well regulated militia, being necessary to the security of a free state, the right of the people to keep and bear arms, shall not be infringed."

Contrary to popular political beliefs, the right to possess a firearm has little to do with hunting or any other recreational activity. The basic right to possess a gun serves a much more important function in our society: self-defense. The right has two purposes: It allows individuals to protect themselves from criminals when the government is *unable to protect* them. Even more importantly, the right exists so that individuals can protect themselves *from the government* when it unjustly attacks them.

Over the last hundred years, federal and state governments have engaged in a direct assault on the right to possess firearms. Legislators have enacted law after law in order to eradicate the right slowly. These so-called gun controls make it extraordinarily difficult for a law-abiding individual to obtain a weapon and nearly impossible for that person to carry and actually use the weapon in self-defense.

When the government strips persons of their right to protect themselves and gets away with it, a dangerous precedent is established. America is spiraling downward on a slippery slope toward a defenseless population. An interesting aside, when James Madison proposed the Bill of Rights, the Second Amendment was the least debated amendment.

The Nazis used gun control to disarm the Jews in Eastern Europe. In a matter of hours on November 9, 1938—Kristallnacht—the Nazis killed at least 91 Jews, injured countless others,[18] destroyed 7,500 Jewish businesses,[19] and burned 267 synagogues.[20] The Nazis arrested about 30,000 Jews and transported them to concentration camps.[21] But people able to hold on to their weapons and exercise their basic right to self-defense were much more successful in resisting the Nazi genocide. Consider the Warsaw Ghetto uprising of April 1943. A loosely organized group of Zionists, the Jewish Combat Organization (ZOB) never totaled more than 220 individuals[22] who were ill equipped to fight the Nazis. But with only small arms and grenades, they were able to kill about three hundred members of the German military and hold them off for almost a month. If German citizens had been able to maintain arms and fight for their lives like members of the ZOB did, then perhaps six million Jews would never have suffered their tragic and horrific fate.

As another example, like the Germans in Hitler's time, the Chinese today are forbidden to own any firearms or ammunition. In 1996, the Chinese government imposed a blanket ban and outlawed the private manufacturing, sale, transportation, possession, importation, or exportation of bullets, guns, and replicated guns. The irony is that as the Chinese government continues to disarm its citizens, it makes a fortune off of the arms trade.[23]

Why would a government making large profits exporting arms prevent its people from owning these arms? The answer is simple: to retain power. As Mao Zedong famously remarked, "Political power grows out of the barrel of a gun."

Unfortunately, despite what we are taught, our own nation's history of gun laws is more similar to Eastern Europe's and China's history than we would like to believe. Currently, the federal government reaps the tax and trade benefits of our nation being the number one producer and exporter of arms, yet restricts the right of its citizens to keep and bear arms.[24]

This disarming of American individuals is not new. During the period after the Civil War, Southern governments enacted Black Codes that prohibited freed slaves and all blacks from owning and bearing firearms. By disarming the former slaves, it became virtually impossible for them to defend themselves from the violent actions of the KKK.

Statutes such as those enacted after the Civil War and in subsequent periods are exactly the atrocities the Second Amendment and Fourteenth Amendment were meant to prevent. If we are unable to learn the lessons history offers us, we are fools destined to repeat the mistakes of those who have gone before us.

The Gun Control Act of 1968 and the Omnibus Crime Control and Safe Streets Act required all gun owners to be over the age of eighteen and prohibited the sales of arms between residents of different states. Moreover, a gun-licensing program was implemented and a manipulative "sporting test" was developed. Yet, after allegations of abuse and a complete about-face by the government, the Firearms Owners Protection Act of 1986 was enacted.

By 1993, though, the government was up to its old tricks, and President Clinton signed into law the Brady Handgun Violence Prevention Act on November 30. The main purpose of the Brady Act was to provide "for a [five-day] waiting period before the purchase of a handgun, and for the establishment of a national instant criminal background check system to be contacted by firearms dealers before the transfer of any firearm."[25] This act expired on November 30, 1998, and the waiting period ceased to apply when the computerized instant check system came online.

Then, in 1994, the government enacted the Violent Crime Control Act, or, more appropriately, the Federal Assault Weapons Ban. This act was designed to prohibit the sale of specified semiautomatic firearms (labeled "assault weapons") to civilians. The act designated nineteen weapons as assault weapons and then provided a definition of assault weapons based on certain senseless combinations of a variety of nonlethal features.

By creating gun bans and stripping you of your natural right to protect your personal property, the government is not keeping you any safer. Rather, the government is giving criminals more firepower for their crimes, as revealed by a close analysis of the numbers—numbers that the government continually chooses to ignore.

When individuals assert their fundamental human right of self-defense, government officials are often outraged; a tyrannical government is not happy with the power to employ violence in the hands of the people, rather than monopolized in the hands of the government.

Ronald Dixon, a Jamaican immigrant and a US Navy veteran, legally purchased a gun in Florida and was in the process of registering it in Brooklyn, New York, where he lives. On the night of December 14, 2002, Dixon was awakened by sounds of a burglar in his home. He saw an intruder enter the bedroom of his two-year-old son. He used his gun to fire two shots into the intruder's chest. The intruder, Ivan Thompson, had five previous felony convictions; his fourteen-page rap sheet included numerous instances of burglary and larceny.

Dixon did nothing more than exercise his natural right to protect his family against a vile human being who meant them harm, yet Brooklyn District Attorney Charles Hynes decided to make him into a criminal. Dixon faced a penalty of up to one year imprisonment, after being arrested for illegally possessing a handgun. Hynes, displaying logic that would outrage even a first-grader, proclaimed, "We're not disputing that Mr. Dixon had a right to shoot the person who broke into his house. But he had no right to have that gun."

What was he to shoot the invader with, Mr. Hynes? Did Hynes expect Dixon to watch the intruder murder his two-year-old and pray that the police show up in time? Or should Dixon have called Hynes to expedite his gun registration before he pulled the trigger?

Who in their right mind would not use a gun under these circumstances to save an innocent, defenseless baby?

After national outrage among members of the media and supporters of the Second Amendment, led by my Fox News colleague Sean Hannity, Hynes agreed to let Dixon escape jail time by pleading guilty to a "disorderly conduct" violation. Even though Dixon never went to jail, the State of New York clearly violated his Second Amendment rights. His life never should have been disrupted by the district attorney, he never should have been threatened with imprisonment for exercising a natural right, and he should not have had to incur legal expenses.

Do guns create or prevent harm?

Year after year, the statistics prove that *more guns mean less crime*. In other words, the number of gun crimes committed lessens as prohibitions on guns are weakened. Yet our government officials continuously preach the myth that guns create, instead of prevent, harm.

Currently, there are approximately 300 million privately owned firearms in the US, and nearly 100 million are handguns. On average, the number of firearms rises by more than 4 million annually. There are about 70 to 80 million gun owners in the United States, which is about 40 to 45 percent of all American households.[26] The reality is that almost every year, guns kill about 30,000 Americans, and about 1,000 of these deaths are accidental. While these numbers appear staggering, fewer than 2 percent of handguns and 1 percent of all guns in this country will ever be used to commit a violent crime.[27] Thus, the use of blanket prohibitions against owning guns is like burning a haystack to get to a needle.

THE RIGHT TO PETITION THE GOVERNMENT

What are the historical roots of the right to petition the government?

History demonstrates that when grievances go unanswered, the aggrieved will inevitably seek to overthrow those in power. In other words, the alternative to the right to petition has been violent regime change. In fact, many historians posit that Britain was able to avoid the bloody revolutions on the European continent in the eighteenth and nineteenth centuries because the right to petition secured for the people a participatory role in government. The stability of the political system was largely based upon the ability of the king's subjects to request that certain actions be taken and the corresponding expectation that, in response to those petitions, the king would evenhandedly redress their grievances.

The right to petition furthers popular sovereignty by making the government accountable to the people for all of its wrongs and misguided policies: petitions are demands made by the masters (the people) to their servants (the government). If we lose the ability to petition the government, we also lose our right to demand that the government protect our freedoms instead of merely enhance its own power. In the colonies, the right to petition the government was deemed so essential a right that it was one of the few guaranteed to those traditionally disenfranchised members of society, to women, Indians, and even slaves. What could be a more fundamental human yearning than freely and uninhibitedly to right wrongs that have been committed against us?

Moreover, it is the right to petition the government from which other First Amendment rights, such as speech and assembly, are made more effective. Specifically, for instance, if the right to petition is to be truly absolute, then the people compiling those petitions need to be able to assemble and speak freely. Also, the right to petition the government is the right by which most other rights are protected. After all, the Constitution cannot defend itself; its provisions will only ever take effect through the constant vigilance of those who wish to remain free.

One more note. One of the principal reasons that America declared its independence was the British government's refusal to hear petitions from the colonies. So when the Founders incorporated into the Constitution the right to petition, they also enshrined its essential protections, namely, the prohibition of penalties for petitioning and the duty of the government to respond.

The two kinds of petitions serve different interests. The first is the traditional legislative petition, which typically comes in the form of a letter sent to one's representatives. Activists draft this letter and gather signatures. The second is the judicial petition, which is essentially a lawsuit against the government.

The legislative petition—the first kind—ensures government accountability to the people. Citizens are free "to question the legality of the government's actions, to present their views on controversial matters, and to demand that the government, as the servant of the people, be responsive to the popular will."[28]

Sometimes, however, petitions do more than request that government do something differently. Instead, these petitions argue that the government has violated an established legal right. Imagine the difference between petitioning the government to build a road around Boston instead of New York and petitioning the government to release you from unlawful imprisonment. In the latter case, you actually have a legal right to be free from that kind of action, and if that right is transgressed, then you are able to sue the offending party in court for a remedy. Such judicial petitions were especially important in early America because individuals distrusted legislatures and favored the neutrality offered by an independent judiciary. The Founders recognized the danger of the government being a judge in its own cause.

Thus, at the time of the founding, the petition clause included both the right to sue the government and the right to request the government to take or abandon a particular action. Both were based upon the desire for government accountability to the people and the resolution of disputes by a neutral arbiter, and both are essential features of liberty.

Is our right to petition compromised by our government's declaration of immunity?

Yes. Despite the crucial role that the right to petition plays in our constitutional system, the government has managed to shield itself from judicial petitions via the doctrine of sovereign immunity. Why can the government say when it will be sued and when it will not be? What is the basis for treating a government that harms innocent persons differently from businesses and individuals who harm innocent persons? As you may have guessed, sovereign immunity cannot be reconciled with the right to petition the government judicially for redress of grievances. With this doctrine of sovereign immunity, the government has eviscerated the right to petition and therefore escapes accountability to the people for its violations of the law. The doctrine of sovereign immunity violates the Natural Law by suggesting that the temporal (in this case, a man-made government) is superior to the immutable principles of nature.

Interestingly, the original justifications for the notion of government accountability to the law was that government is the "fountain and head of justice and equity," so we can assume that the government would consent to having those wrongs redressed. Surely the government would not mind being sued if doing so would accomplish its true purpose: justly protecting our freedoms. Thus, there can be no legitimate reason why government should remain immune from continuous accountability.

Why, then, does the government insist upon sovereign immunity? The answer lies in what St. Augustine referred to as *libido dominandi*, the lust to dominate, the desire to exert control over others. And there is no better example of *libido dominandi* than the government's evisceration of the judicial petition, in direct contempt of God and Natural Law. When the government escapes justice, not only are innocents harmed, but the escape establishes a precedent for future governments to do the same.

Rule 11 is a federal civil procedure that allows the government to punish petitioners. When asked how this rule can be reconciled with the right to petition, one of the drafters simply responded, "There is no constitutional right to make frivolous petitions."

First, "frivolous" and "well researched" are not the same thing, and Rule 11 only punishes those petitions that are inadequately researched rather than those that are genuinely frivolous. In other words, the government will punish those petitions that are meritorious, but have not been adequately researched. But this threat of fines can deter otherwise meritorious claims, particularly when those claims are novel or controversial. This is often the case for suits against the government, since petitioners are frequently challenging a traditional and entrenched governmental practice.

It is high time, however, that we abolish Rule 11 and, rather than punish petitioners, encourage them to take up their grievances with the government and modify the existing law. So why have Rule 11 motions remained the law? A federal judge once said that "insubstantial lawsuits against high public officials . . . warrant firm application of

[Rule 11 because they] undermine the effectiveness of Government." But the effectiveness of government should *never* trump the need for the robust protection of our constitutional rights.

THE RIGHT TO ENJOY PEACE

Why does any president want to go to war?

The truth is that the ultimate crisis—war—is a dear friend of the state. In fact, the government uses war as the ultimate means to expand its own power, size, and scope. And it does so in a multitude of ways: tax and budget increases, security laws and regulations, nationalization of industry, censorship of speech and expression, suspension of due process, warrantless searches and seizures, and blanket arrests of war resisters.[29] Every single one of these measures grossly swells the size and scope of government, thereby stripping us of the freedom to live as we please.

More fundamentally, however, war is the most effective assertion of the primacy of the collective over the individual. The state *needs* warfare in order to continue its existence as a coercive force intruding upon our lives. War is the state's way of saying, "I am still important and am owed your continuing support and allegiance."

Why could the bloodiest war in American history — the Civil War — have been avoided, and how did Abraham Lincoln increase federal power and assault the Constitution?

L incoln claimed that the Civil War was about emancipating slaves, but he could have simply paid slave owners to set their slaves free. The benefits of the Union would have been fairly easy to see once a few Southern states tried to go it alone for a bit. But Lincoln chose not to compensate slave owners and thereby end the dreaded institution. Instead he chose to deny states their right to participate voluntarily in the Union.

Lincoln's actions were unconstitutional, and he knew it. Before running for president, Lincoln was quoted as saying that the Southern states would not be permitted to secede (not, significantly, that they did not have a *right* to secede). By barring their departure, Lincoln preserved the geographical Union but tore apart the Constitution. He blatantly ignored the rights of the states to secede from the Union, a right that is clearly implicit in the Constitution, since it was the *states* that ratified the Constitution and thereby decided to enter the Union. Surely these same states had the right to decide to undo that act. The right to secede from any confederation, group, or union is derived from the Natural Law of freedom to associate.

Why is the legendary term "Honest Abe" not so accurate?

Federalism has been called one of the greatest contributions of the Founding Fathers to the field of government—and Lincoln singlehandedly voided that contribution. Professor Thomas DiLorenzo has said:

> The federal government will never check its own power. That is the whole reason for federalism and the reason the founding fathers adopted a federal system of government. . . . There is no check at all on the federal government unless state sovereignty exists, and state sovereignty is itself meaningless without the right of secession. Thus Lincoln's war, by destroying the right of secession, also destroyed the last check on the potentially tyrannical power of the central state."[30]

And DiLorenzo is correct. Lincoln destroyed federalism through the Civil War.

One more point. By the time of the Civil War, many foreign countries had ended slavery peacefully. England had freed its slaves without a violent conflict about twenty years earlier. Gradual emancipation would be successful in the Dutch colonies (1863), Puerto Rico (1873), Brazil (1871–88), and Cuba (1886).[31] To this day, the Civil War has the distinction of having the highest death toll of American citizens of any conflict in which the United States has been a part.[32]

A braham Lincoln was committed to taxing Americans to the fullest extent of their tolerance, and he would not let the Constitution stand in his way. Lincoln's tax policies were not in the best interests of a free democratic nation. From 1861 to 1865, duties on imports were increased several times per year. The tax rate on imports was almost 50 percent by 1862. This was said to serve the interests of domestic producers, mainly Northern domestic producers who financed the activities of the Republican Party.

During the war, and under Lincoln's leadership, the first income tax was imposed (the Revenue Act of 1861). Additionally, tax rates on occupational licensing, stamps, and inheritance were also increased. This expanded the reach of the federal government. National banks were established under the National Currency Acts of 1863 and 1864. They competed with, and bankrupted, many state banks.

Under Lincoln, Congress enacted the Homestead Act of 1862, which gave away 270 million acres of public land to private citizens. Anyone who was at least twenty-one years of age could receive a parcel of 160 acres if he lived on the land and improved it for five years. The Homestead Act encouraged many people to settle in the West, but where was the constitutional authority to do this?

Lincoln increased the power of the federal government at the expense of the rights of the states and civil liberties. This opened the door to more unconstitutional acts by the government in the 1900s through to today.

After the Civil War ended, as industrialization was changing the nature of the national economy, Congress passed many new federal economic regulations. The Sherman Antitrust Act of 1890 and the Interstate Commerce Act of 1887 inaugurated a new era of federal legislation.

But that legislation ran into a roadblock. Scholars and judges of this period increasingly espoused a belief in laissez-faire principles, whereby less government interference in the free markets would make for a better system. Between 1887 and 1937, the Supreme Court championed these principles. The justices ruled that the Constitution, by its recognition of private property, freedom to contract, and due process, dictated that the federal government should not play a role in regulating the economy. This was in part due to the Court's continued belief in Natural Law principles.

Under Natural Law, the freedom to trade is an important right of all human beings. The Constitution explicitly prohibits the states and by implication the federal government from interfering with private contracts. We see the aggressive use of judicial review, but this time to uphold the natural rights of individuals by restraining the government from interfering with them.

When have presidents lied to rally support for a war?

A brief examination of our country's short history demonstrates that many presidents have used self-created fear and hysteria to justify war.

- To garner American support for the Spanish-American War, President William McKinley touted the sinking of the USS *Maine*. McKinley claimed that a Spanish mine caused the boat's destruction, when—according to the ship's American captain—a coal bin explosion caused the boat's sinking.

- President Woodrow Wilson created the illusion that his soon-to-be World War I enemy—Germany—fired the first shot at the United States, when in reality Germany had notified the US that the British passenger ship, the *Lusitania*, carried illegal weapons and would become a German target in open waters. When the *Lusitania* went down near the coast of Ireland, 114 Americans went down with it.

- Franklin Delano Roosevelt was eager to fight the Germans, but he recognized that Americans were still reeling from World War I and the Great Depression. So he promised US citizens neutrality even as he planned to provoke the Japanese navy into killing American sailors, forcing him to respond militarily. FDR sent US ships into Japanese waters on so-called "pop-up" missions, and the US issued an ultimatum to Japan to remove all ships from China and Indochina.

The United States continued to monitor Japanese communications, but consciously chose not to prevent the attack. Eventually, FDR's strategy paid off—and the cost was 2,403 Americans dead from the Japanese attack on Pearl Harbor and 405,399 Americans eventually killed in World War II.

- President Lyndon B. Johnson provoked an attack to spark the Vietnam War, claiming that America was shot at first. To carry out his charade, President Johnson pushed through a pliant Congress the Gulf of Tonkin Resolution—which was itself based on false reports of attacks on American naval forces.

- As for the War on Terror, George W. Bush purposefully inspired fear and anxiety in Americans through every channel of communication available to him. Bush and his team, not having presented any convincing evidence of so-called weapons of mass destruction, lied us into war with Iraq. If the government truly believed that we were all in grave danger, if terrorists were lingering in our airports, then surely it would shift all of its resources toward eliminating that threat. So why was Congress spending money on fertilizer (the $180 billion farm bill in 2002), math books ($40 billion), job training programs, and peonies ($11 billion annually for "community development programs"[33])?

None of Roosevelt's, McKinley's, Wilson's, FDR's, Johnson's, or Bush's actions were morally, legally, or constitutionally justified.

While war is being fought abroad in the name of freedom, war brings the opposite effect to Americans back home: we are *less* free because of war. While this statement may seem contradictory, consider the higher taxes, greater government debt, increased government intrusion in markets, more pervasive government surveillance, and the manipulation and control of the public.[34]

The most tried and true way of limiting Americans' freedom during times of war is the draft. President Wilson drafted almost 2.8 million men during World War I.[35] This involuntary servitude—a violation of all natural rights—was found to be constitutional by the Supreme Court at the time, a prime example of how crisis allows people to pull off unconstitutional measures.

What civil liberties suffer during wartime?

For starters, the government implemented the Espionage Act of June 1917 to silence critics of the draft. Penalizing willful obstruction of enlistment services with fines of $10,000 and imprisonment as long as twenty years, the federal government stripped away both freedom of speech and religion. The feds also censored all printed materials, deported aliens, and encouraged warrantless searches and seizures. People were even arrested for reading the Bill of Rights and the Constitution in public.[36]

Almost a century later, the PATRIOT Act creates some of the same consequences. It lets the government snoop around our private communications and personal records. It expands the size and power of federal agencies and allows searches and seizures of our property without a warrant or even probable cause. The PATRIOT Act also permits the president to detain us without counsel for indefinite periods. Whatever happened to the freedoms the Constitution was written to guarantee?

What economic liberties suffer during wartime?

Controls on business during both World War I and World War II severely restricted Americans' economic freedoms. The feds "nationalized the railroad, telephone, domestic telegraph, and international telegraphic cable industries," asserting control over prices, people, and corporations.[37] Regulations in the forms of manipulation of "labor-management regulations, securities sales, agricultural production and marketing, the distribution of coal and oil, international commerce, and markets for raw materials and manufactured products" highly constricted private enterprise and free market practices.[38]

Moreover, unnecessary agencies are created during wars. Typically, they grow in size and lengthen the list of regulations under which we live. After war, some disappear, while others magically morph into the "solution" of other government problems.

The ultimate theft and restriction of property is the government's withholding of income taxes, a practice not implemented until World War II and wholly unsupported by our Founding Fathers. In an effort to raise funds for the war effort, Congress passed the Revenue Act of 1942. This act imposed a "Victory Tax" on income: that tax was to be withheld by the employer and paid directly to the government. Gradually this practice increased in scope to constitute the present system of income taxation in America.

There are several evils inherent in this practice. First, by allowing the government to seize property directly and send the taxpayer back any surplus, it portrays the government as a beneficent caretaker. Second, it deprives the taxpayer of the use of his money for a period of time, and that money could have flowed into investments and generated a return while the government was holding on to it. Finally, this system of taxation enables the government to increase in size, as it would be infinitely more difficult to wrest tax dollars from the taxpayers themselves than secreting them away from their employer. And this system of taxation was all made possible because of war. Constitutionally and philosophically, withholding taxes presumes that we exist to serve the government rather than vice versa.

THE RIGHT TO FAIRNESS FROM THE GOVERNMENT

What procedural requirements are most essential for the protection of individual liberties?

O ur basic freedoms cannot be taken away by the government unless we are convicted of violating Natural Law, and the government can only convict us if it follows what is called "procedural due process." *Due process* means that we know in advance of violations of Natural Law that the government will prosecute, that we are fully notified by the government of the charges against us, that we have a fair trial with counsel before a truly neutral judge and jury, that we can confront and challenge the government's evidence against us, that we can summon persons and evidence on our own behalf, that the government must prove our misdeeds beyond a reasonable doubt, and that we have the right to appeal the outcome of that trial to another neutral judge.

The need for due process arises out of the fact that there are circumstances where the government can, and should, lawfully deprive people of their liberty. After all, if one person does harm to another, that is, "an intentional physical invasion or aggression of another person's body or rights or property," then, under those limited circumstances, the government is right in prosecuting that individual. This concept is a waiver of rights: the thief or invader, by his theft or aggression, waives the permanency and inalienability of his own natural rights by violating the natural rights of another. The government can never deprive a person of his rights to life, liberty, and property; when the government prosecutes a genuinely guilty individual, these rights were already waived by him and by him alone. This is simply an application of the principle of personal responsibility.

The government, however, can wrongly use this power to prosecute an individual improperly, to punish the wrong person and thereby eviscerate any meaningful protection of his substantive rights. In short, there must be some scheme of procedural constraints to ensure that our natural rights are actually enforced and that liberty is deprived only when its possessor has given up his own rights by his own actions.

C ities and municipalities determine that they could use a little extra cash, so they implement traffic enforcement cameras at major intersections. These "scameras," upon determining that you commit a red light infraction, take a picture of your car and mail you a citation. These cameras do not increase public safety; they only allow the government to convict you illegally of a crime that you may not have committed.

Take San Diego, California, a city that in 1998 was in need of $100 million for maintenance of roads and other public works. In 1998, San Diego officials entered into a contract with Lockheed Martin IMS Corp. Lockheed Martin paid for the installation of nineteen cameras, and operated the system. San Diego would receive $271 for each traffic conviction, of which Lockheed Martin would receive $70. So the manufacturer had a financial incentive to create a camera designed not only to capture speeders, but also to convict them.

In eighteen months, one camera alone generated $6.8 million in revenue. Given such incentive, it's no big surprise that testimony presented to the House Subcommittee on Highways and Safety revealed the city's traffic camera program was a complete scam intended only for increased revenues, concocted "under the guise of public safety."

Lockheed Martin and San Diego claimed that the cameras would save lives, but not a single report substantiates this claim. Of the thousands of photos taken by Lockheed Martin's cameras, not a single photo shows a red light violator causing a collision.

Shockingly, officials from Lockheed Martin, not from San Diego, chose the intersections for the nineteen cameras. Lockheed Martin selected the locations not based on safety, but on revenue potential. Not only did Lockheed Martin have an incentive to issue more citations, but the contract also allowed its officials to remove the camera from an intersection when there was a 25 percent decrease in the number of citations issued.

It was later determined that, at three intersections, Lockheed Martin illegally moved the censor that measures whether the car crosses into the intersection during a red light so as *to increase the likelihood* of a conviction.

Numerous studies show that the most effective way to reduce red light violations—and traffic accidents—is to increase the yellow light interval. When one San Diego intersection's yellow light interval was increased from 3.0 to 4.7 seconds, the number of monthly red light violations dropped from 2,265 to 205! As former San Diego Mayor

Roger Hedgecock testified to Congress, there was "not a single scrap of evidence that one life has been saved" by the cameras. Additionally, Hedgecock explained that San Diego was "contracting out law enforcement [to private, for-profit, corporations]. Outrageous."

Americans have an inalienable right to life, liberty, and property; the government may not strip individuals of these rights without due process. In San Diego, the government devised an elaborate and devious scheme to convict harmless and innocent people. When the yellow light interval becomes so small that it is inevitable that you will run a red light, as was the case at some San Diego intersections, the government is entrapping you: it is *facilitating* and *inducing* you to the break the law. If the government caused the duration of the yellow light to become one second or less, it would be *forcing* you to commit a crime! With no fair process whatsoever, the government has deprived drivers in San Diego of their liberty (by convicting them of a crime) and their property (by robbing them of $271 per citation).

The judiciary has not acted as an effective check on law enforcement's use of scameras. In 2001, three hundred violators had their citations dismissed by San Diego Superior Court Judge Ronald Styn, who ruled that a private company had too much involvement, and the city had too little involvement, in the process. In other words, *the government* was not enforcing the law, *Lockheed Martin* was. Sadly, Judge Styn is a rare exception.

While cameras don't lie, government officials do. A driver who is automatically mailed a red light violation has no effective way of establishing that the government rigged the system. The Sixth Amendment guarantees the right to confront one's accuser. How can an individual cross-examine the camera? While an individual can certainly spend numerous hours reviewing traffic documentation and reports to prove his innocence, the government knows that most individuals have not the time, ability, or money to do so. So, the government collects a little $271 check from you, when you did little wrong, and there is little you can do about it!

J *udicial review* is the power of the Supreme Court, and eventually all federal courts, to examine a statute (and eventually the behavior of the president and the states as well) and to declare it void if the Court finds it to run counter to the Constitution.

Justice John Marshall wrote that "it is the very essence of judicial duty to decide if two laws conflict, which shall supersede, and whether any law conflicts with the Constitution, which is superior and must prevail." This entire argument is brilliant, rational, and consistent with the Natural Law principle that the creature (the Congress) cannot negate acts of its creator (the Constitution).

Public necessity and expediency are to be enforced by means of judicial review. When learned judges have adequately scrutinized our officials' commands and determined that they stem from the Constitution and that they do not infringe upon our natural rights, only then are those laws legitimate, giving rise to our moral obligation to obey them.

Sadly, judicial scrutiny of legislative and executive commands has been woefully inadequate, allowing our natural rights to be circumvented time and again. Take, for example, the case of *United States v. Carolene Products*

(1938), in which the Court reasoned that a statute should be *presumed* constitutional and thus the burden was on the defendant to prove that Congress could have no constitutional authority and no lawful basis for the regulations it had set in place. This was not a protection of the defendant's liberty. Why should the individual—rather than the governmental officials who gathered and relied upon data in crafting policy—have the burden of both finding and presenting that evidence? It is inefficient as well as unrealistic and unjust to place this burden on the individual. But might the government have secured and advanced this presumption of constitutionality—and the concomitant burden of disproving it upon the persons whose liberties the government itself has violated—in order to assure its maintenance and possession of its coercive powers? In a word, *yes*. The individual will undoubtedly have inadequate access to relevant information, thus increasing the chance that he will lose even when evidence clearly and convincingly shows that the statute was in fact unconstitutional.

While the act of passing a fair law satisfies one requirement of due process—substantive due process—there is another part of due process: fair hearings in neutral courts, preceded by ample notice of litigation and an opportunity to appeal. This is called procedural due process: the government can under no circumstances deprive one of life, liberty, or property without litigating that action in courts. Without the accused having access to fair hearings, the propriety of a government action is entirely the opinion of the very government that took that action. In order to ensure that a person is deprived of liberty only when genuinely warranted, that deprivation must take place in a neutral court and involve the following elements: notice, hearing, fairness, and a right of appeal. These elements are as old as our legal culture, and as has been proven over time, each is essential before a deprivation of liberty can be considered proper. The right of appeal plays a crucial role by ensuring that judgments are in fact correct and that a litigant was not the victim of a judge's improvident behavior.

Furthermore, without a jury, litigants would be at the mercy of a corrupt or prejudiced judge. Similar to the situations that arise when laws are vague, a judge could determine guilt for nearly any reason he wished, regardless of the accused's actual guilt or innocence. Also, judges possess a bias by virtue of being appointed by some machinery in the government, and this bias is mitigated by the presence of a jury comprised of the people themselves. In essence, without a jury there could be no such thing as the separation of powers, and the government would be, in the words of James Madison, "a judge in its own cause." Finally and not insignificantly, juries will oftentimes be more faithful to the Natural Law and its principles of justice rather than simply acting according to whatever is customary and dictated by precedent.

The crucial protection provided by juries (and procedural due process) has parallels in other political institutions as well, resulting in what I collectively refer to as "tripartite nullification." In addition to jury nullification of state prosecutors, the states retain the power to nullify the unconstitutional behavior of the federal government. Under this concept, states are obligated to refrain from enforcing unconstitutional federal laws. Third, individuals should have the right to withdraw their consent from state and local government, in effect nullifying governmental actions taken in violation of their natural rights.

This tripartite nullification should sound familiar. It is, in essence, checks and balances between federal, state, and local governments *and* the people themselves. What would happen if checks and balances were wholly eliminated at the federal level of government? What if the Supreme Court could no longer strike down laws as unconstitutional, the president himself could declare war, and Congress could pass any legislation without fear of an executive veto or a judicial invalidation? Government would expand even further than it has already. Tripartite nullification is essential to keeping government within its proper scope. Sadly, however, it has been wholly ignored.

THE RIGHT TO SOUND MONEY

Where are the roots of the secrecy, conspiracy, and fraud we find in today's banking?

A goldsmith's original job was to transform gold extracted from the earth into coins of equal weight and value. They had very secure buildings in which to store the gold, safe from the reach of thieves. Since people also began to stockpile these highly valuable metals for future security, they, too, had to protect their gold from thieves, so they kept their gold in the goldsmiths' vaults—for a fee, of course. In return for depositing their gold in the goldsmiths' vaults, the people received a certificate that was a claim for the amount of gold they had stored in the vaults. Rather than receiving the very same gold they had taken to the goldsmith, the depositors would be given its precise equivalent. Since it was very inconvenient to go back and forth continually to the goldsmiths' vaults to claim their gold in order to trade at the market, people started leaving their gold in the vaults and trading the claim certificates.

When goldsmiths realized this, they saw an opportunity. If most people were leaving their gold in the vaults for safe-keeping, goldsmiths typically did not have to worry about exchanging all the gold in their vaults all at once for claim checks. They could instead start loaning out claim checks for a fee (interest)—and they could do so for more gold than they actually had in their vaults. If someone wanted to claim his own gold or see if there was actually gold in the vault, he could do so: there was still enough there to make good on the small day-to-day transactions. When people became aware of this fraud, they panicked and frequently rushed to the goldsmith to claim their gold only to find out they had been conned and there was not enough gold to be claimed for all the outstanding claim checks. People were furious to have been robbed of their hard-earned gold, furious because their natural rights to property had been violated. Are you seeing the secrecy and fraud? Now for some conspiracy.

Kings and governments saw great opportunity with this claim-check system since it created an institution that could provide massive funding for projects and wars that would expand their empires and increase their power. So government-sponsored fractional reserve banking was born. Since government-chartered banks were able to loan out more currency than they had in their vaults as reserves, there still remained a possibility of a bank run. In an attempt to mitigate this possibility, governments created "lenders of last resort": a government-sponsored and privately owned central bank that would control the issuance of all currency within their nation. If banks suffered a run, they could always turn to the central bank for immediate loans to keep them in business. In other words, this system of central banking propped up the fraud highlighted above. Like any action that has the capacity to violate the Natural Law, this power should never have been given to a person, institution, or government.

Thomas Jefferson and James Madison definitely saw the fraud, and they had the courage to stand against it. The first central bank in America—the First Bank of the United States—was chartered to pay off debts accrued during the Revolutionary War. This bank spread the debt evenly among the colonies and was relatively small, controlling only about 20 percent of the nation's money supply. Jefferson, however, was not fooled into believing the bank's influence would remain this small and wisely allowed the bank's charter to expire.

Five years later, in 1816, Congress chartered the Second Bank of the United States, and President James Madison signed it into law. This second bank's life only lasted until 1833 when President Andrew Jackson allowed the charter to expire after a bank panic. Jackson faced a hard decision: he could let banking institutions fail, causing unemployment in the short term, or he could bail them out with the central bank system, causing erosion in the value of the nation's currency in the long term. Having watched the bankers in action, President Jackson was concerned about funding them with a central bank: Jackson recognized that then the bankers would have an incentive to take as much risk as possible and share the profits amongst themselves but spread the losses amongst the taxpayers as the ultimate "lender of last resort." The future of this country would be brighter had all presidents since Andrew Jackson possessed both his understanding of the dangers of a central bank and the courage necessary to resist its temptations.

About thirty years after Jackson ended the Second Bank of the United States, the debt accumulated by the federal government during the Civil War made a return to a system of central banking extremely attractive to the Lincoln administration. This debt prompted Congress to pass and President Lincoln to sign the National Banking Acts of 1863 and 1864. Although the American economy continued to grow despite being dominated by this third system of central banking, it nonetheless saw great turbulence with many boom-and-bust cycles and bank panics. In 1873, 1893, 1901, and 1907, massive panics caused a series of bank failures, proving how unstable this central system of banking was.

B ank customers have a lot to lose.

First of all, realize that banks pushed for centralization of control with a government backing or a government-backed banking cartel. With this cartel, the commercial banks could utilize cheap—sometimes free—loans from the central bank, so the commercial bank would have access to all the money it needed both to conduct daily transactions and honor legal claims in the event of a bank run. Moreover, the government set up an insurance system, the Federal Deposit Insurance Corporation (FDIC), to protect deposit accounts from the risk of losses. The FDIC is funded, of course, by taxpayer dollars.

If the banks received government backing, they would then be able to profit from their gains and pass their losses along to the taxpayers in the form of bailouts, just as President Andrew Jackson warned about and predicted 180 years ago. Big government, constantly needing money to fund its military adventurism, welfare state, and campaigns for more power, would clearly benefit from this system, as would the cartel members. Everyone else, by contrast, would be outright robbed of their savings through inflation.

What is the Federal Reserve Act?

On November 22, 1910, Senator Nelson W. Aldrich (R-RI) and five companions set forth under assumed names in a privately chartered railroad car from Hoboken, New Jersey, to Jekyll Island, Georgia, allegedly on a duck-hunting expedition. Once at the island, these powerful banking elites would devise the new central banking system and draft what is now known as the Aldrich Plan. This plan was defeated in 1912, but it formed the substance of the Federal Reserve Act which was passed in 1913. Professor Murray N. Rothbard describes this system:

> The Fed was given a monopoly of the issue of all bank notes; national banks, as well as state banks, could now only issue deposits, and the deposits had to be redeemable in Federal Reserve Notes as well as, at least nominally, in gold. All national banks were "forced" to become members of the Federal Reserve System, a "coercion" they had long eagerly sought. This meant that national bank reserves had to be kept in the form of demand deposits, or checking accounts, at the Fed. The Fed was now in place as lender of last resort. With the prestige, power, and resources of the US Treasury solidly behind it, it could inflate more

consistently than the Wall Street banks under the National Banking System. Above all, it could and did inflate even during recessions in order to bail out the banks. The Fed could now try to keep the economy from recessions that liquidated the unsound investments of the inflationary boom, and it could try to keep the inflation going indefinitely.[39]

The Federal Reserve would cause the first Great Depression only fifteen years later.

T he evils of the Federal Reserve System (the Fed) run so deep that its proponents understand that its operations must take place in *full secrecy*. This fact, in tandem with the current financial crisis, has recently prompted calls for the organization to be more transparent. Yet the belief is that once we, the American people, become aware of what these central bankers are clandestinely doing with our hard-earned money, we will demand an end to the Fed.

Since the institution of the secret Federal Reserve in 1913, the US dollar has lost about 93 percent of its value, and the US economy has seen countless boom-and-bust cycles that have destroyed the economy and caused massive unemployment.

When the currency used by our Founding Fathers fell victim to hyperinflation in the early days of the nation, the Constitution made clear that only gold and silver could be used as legal tender. Nonetheless, a simple matter of consti-tutional interpretation—the Constitution was ignored—has instead given rise to a massive system that has handicapped the ability of individuals to exercise their natural right to seek prosperity. The Fed, cloaked in secrecy and esotericism, has offended the Natural Law as surely as any government agency we have yet witnessed.

Normally, banks loan money to the government by purchasing treasury bills. In the past, treasury bills have been one of the safest investments, since the federal government's debt is guaranteed to be repaid with interest by you and me, the taxpayers. The government can then decide what to do with this money, say, funding any one of its special interest projects or even our collective welfare. As you can see, the banks, the government, and the corporations that the government favors benefit from this system, while everyone else is robbed of their purchasing power in order to fund it.

And this inflationary system of theft makes it impossible for the average American to save for his own retirement. Prior to the abandonment of the gold standard, Americans could work, earn gold as their income, and store it in a bank vault where it would appreciate in value all on its own, serving as their retirement safety net. Fed inflationism depreciates people's savings over time, and the busts the Fed creates wipe out the retirement investments people make in the stock market. The Fed, stated simply, is an abomination to both the Natural Law and the Constitution.

F ifty years ago a movie ticket cost 25 cents; a round-trip subway ticket, 10 cents; a bag of chips, 5 cents; and a soda, 10 cents. A total of 50 cents meant an afternoon of fun. Now going to the movies costs over $16—$10 for a ticket, $2 for the chips, and $4 for the soda—and that's before transportation costs and the tax! This exorbitant increase is a 3,100 percent increase in price! But for some reason people take price increases for granted as a normal occurrence that happens with the passage of time, or they blame the increases on the businesses that charge the higher price, calling them evil and greedy.

But consider what happened to the money supply—the cash in circulation and in bank accounts in the United States—over this same fifty-year period.[40] The increase in the monetary base is the reason for such absurd occurrences as the 3,100 percent increase in the cost of attending a movie. The money supply really started to increase drastically in the mid-1960s. But in 1971, once Nixon took America off the gold standard, money creation grew out of control—and the national debt continues to grow at an outrageous pace.

And every day the federal budget grows, every person loses more and more freedom. The bigger the government, the smaller the amount of individual liberty. Each day of big government is one more day of assaults on our liberties.

Let's look at this. You deposit $1,000 into your checking account. With a 100-percent-reserve banking system, you would just pay a fee to the bank for the safekeeping of your money. Your deposit would mean a decrease in your currency holdings by $1,000 and an increase in your checking account by $1,000: the total money supply in the economy would remain unchanged.[41]

The only way the bank could loan out the funds you deposited without risking a violation of your property rights is if you agree not to withdraw your money for a certain period of time. During this time, you would be free to monitor the loans the bank has given with your money, thus ensuring that the loans are sound and profitable. In this system, banks could never get too big to fail, banks could never collapse an entire economy, and banks could never increase credit to create the bad investments that lead to a boom-and-bust cycle. Moreover, people would never be at risk of losing the money they deposited in their checking accounts; they would only be at risk for the money they voluntarily agreed to allow the bank to loan out. Thus, a 100-percent-reserve system is not only congruent with, but necessary for the enforcement of the Natural Law.

THE RIGHT TO SPEND YOUR OWN MONEY

How is public finance the source of our government's tyranny?

As a starting point, consider the taxes we pay. Because taxation is compulsory, and therefore a forceful taking of our property, we may assume that it is a *malum in se,* an evil in itself. The question then becomes whether there is some valid justification for taxation. As we shall see, no such justification exists, and therefore taxation violates natural property rights. That taxes are justified by some subjective public necessity is an outright lie that we quite literally can no longer afford to believe. Furthermore, the two other means government uses to finance itself—the issuance of public debt and the printing of money—are simply theft by another name and are even more dangerous than taxation. Does the government exist to protect our freedoms, or do we exist to serve the government?

The real tragedy of public finance is that it acts as the great enabler for all of government's most tyrannical actions. How could wars be fought without money? How could we give aid to corrupt regimes without a source of revenue? As

Frank Chodorov warns, "We cannot restore traditional American freedom unless we limit the government's power to tax. No tinkering with this, that, or the other law will stop the trend toward socialism." If we are really, truly committed to the cause of liberty, then we must cut off tyranny at its source: public finance.

What is so inherently evil about taxation?

The basic evil of taxation is that it degrades the individual by flouting his natural rights. In essence, taxation establishes a legal right on the part of the government to your property and to the product of your labor, and the government's right trumps your own. The government's claim of right, however, extends to *all* of your property, not just what it actually takes. Otherwise, the government would not be able to raise taxes whenever it chooses.

In this light, consider the text of the Sixteenth Amendment, passed in 1913: "The Congress shall have power to lay and collect taxes on incomes, from whatever source derived, without apportionment among the several states, and without regard to any census or enumeration." Clearly—and unlike the original Constitution—there are no constitutional restrictions on what Congress may take. Thus, whatever portion of your own property the government declines to take is simply whatever it, in all of its (professed) infinite wisdom and charity, decides you may keep. Our income is no longer a right, and our retained income is but a privilege granted by the government. This arrangement illustrates one of the fundamental legal precepts of socialism: the government decides what it will take from you and what you may keep.

This system of taxation is also the strictest application of legal Positivism: if the government can say when our Natural Rights protect us from aggression and when they do not, then there can be no such thing as Natural Rights. This tenuous, subjective nature of our rights is reflected in the distinction between taxation and theft. *Theft* does not mean a taking of your property, but whatever the government determines to be an *unlawful* taking of your property. Thus, the contemporary understanding of theft is based not on the Natural Law or any ethical principle but on what lawmakers say. Although natural rights and taxation could theoretically be reconciled if free choice were somehow involved, it is in the interest of big government that this will always be an unattainable ideal.

Like taxation, government-issued debt is another of several creative ways our government pays for its initiatives, all of which still amount to theft. If the government chooses not to raise taxes to pay for a program, it can issue a bond: someone agrees to give the government money now in exchange for repayment plus an interest payment at a later date. The problem, however, is that eventually these obligations have to be paid for with taxation. A bond merely allows the government to defer taxation to a later date.

Public debt is theft in the sense that it can only result in more taxation, and thus property will be taken away from you against your will. Public debt is not, however, literally taking money from future generations; clearly, money cannot be "taken" from the future to pay for something today. It is simply reallocated from bondholders to the government, where it is then injected into the economy. For this reason, proponents of bond issuance argue that it is not in fact theft: although future generations will be burdened with a debt obligation on their heads, the money supply will have increased when the government spent the revenues from debt issuance. Thus, this argument goes, there will be more money flowing in the economy with which the future generations can pay those taxes, money that would not have been there but for the issuance.

This argument, however, runs into the same problems we encountered in the discussion of taxation and the social contract. Because future generations obviously cannot consent to pay for government spending when the debt is issued, taxation cannot be in any sense voluntary. Furthermore, it is also unrealistic that future taxpayers will receive benefits commensurate with their tax burden. One group will always be benefitting at the expense of another.

THE RIGHT TO BE GOVERNED BY LAWS WITH MORAL LIMITS

Is the United States government guilty of criminalizing too many behaviors and therefore violating our rights and freedoms?

I would say yes in light of the simple but staggering fact that America has approximately 5 percent of the global population, but 25 percent of the world's prisoners reside here.

Conduct must not merely offend, but cause actual harm in order for the state to seek to punish it as criminal. Moreover, that conduct must be so severe that it can properly be considered harmful not just to the individual, but also to the freedom of all individuals. Any restriction of liberty in the form of criminal punishment is wholly illegitimate unless the exercise of liberty was intended to cause harm and actually did cause harm.

The Constitution offers only extremely limited authorization to criminalize conduct. Thus, only a small fraction of the federal government's criminal code can be considered truly legitimate, and the government—not any individual—is guilty of the greater unlawful conduct. It is high time that we utilize the criminal law for its one and only true purpose: to safeguard our liberties, not restrain them.

Is congressional bribery one way our government does business?

Yes—and I have a couple examples.

First, in 1973, Congress enacted the Emergency Highway Energy Conservation Act as an amendment to the Federal Highway Act. It grants federal funds to the states on the condition that they impose a maximum speed limit of 55 mph on all highways. In 1985, Nevada passed a law that increased its speed limit to 70 mph. Within sixty seconds of the new law coming into effect, the chief of the Nevada division of the Federal Highway Administration advised that the federal Department of Transportation declared that all future funds for state highways would be withheld unless the Nevada speed limit was reduced to 55 mph.

Congress was attempting to bribe the states into doing something indirectly that it could not regulate directly. Nevada argued that because the Highway Act would cut 95 percent of its federal highway funding, the limit violated the "coercion" limitation on the federal spending power.

Second, and briefly, Megan's Law was passed by the federal government, but directs states to develop programs. Any state that fails to operate such a program in compliance with federal standards will face a 10 percent reduction in federal highway funds.

You are probably thinking that if bribery *of*[8] federal officials is illegal, then bribery *by* federal officials should be illegal. How can members of Congress bribe state officials? The point of the federal bribery statute is that they cannot. Yet conditioning the receipt of federal funds on complying with Congress's wishes is essentially bribery with a constitutional fig leaf.

What is legal paternalism
and how does it contribute to the
criminalization of victimless crimes?

The criminalization of victimless offenses is based upon the doctrine of legal paternalism, which is the government's view that it is in a better position to regulate our daily conduct than we are. Wherever this concept prevails, we have the Nanny State (too much salt, too much sugar, hot water too hot, close your windows when your air conditioning is on, etc.). And legal paternalism directly violates the Natural Law principle that no government can be above the individual, since a government is a human creation, and the creature is always subservient to its creator.

To illustrate the practical impropriety of legal paternalism, consider criminal prohibitions on various forms of gambling. At what point in time did the government decide that it is in the best position to tell you how to handle your finances and restrict your ability to gamble? Was it in September of 2007, when our national debt began to rise on an average of $4.13 billion per day?[42] If you were to mimic the government's handling of its finances, how balanced would your budget be?

At any point in time, it is astonishing how many criminal codes we are subject to. You want to jaywalk to make your dentist appointment on time? You can't. You want to sit on a park bench and eat your dinner after sunset? You can't. You want to ride your bike to the grocery store without lugging along a helmet? You can't. You want to skateboard in front of the courthouse? You can't. You want to bet money with your favorite bookie on your favorite baseball team? You can't. You want to buy a drug not approved by the FDA? You can't. You want to cool off with a beer on the beach? You can't. You want to talk on your cell phone while driving safely? You can't. You want to paint the fire hydrant (on your property) in front of your house green to match the grass? You can't. You are on an empty subway car and you want to put your packages on the seat next to you? You can't. You want to collect rainwater on your own property for your own consumption? You can't. Every law, regulation, rule, and ordinance made by the state affects your behavior in some way, and the government has more control over you than you could ever imagine. Such control may seem like a small issue today, but it could end up being more invasive tomorrow.

THE RIGHT TO IGNORE THE STATE

What is the final and capstone natural right?

S ince the government derives its powers from the consent of the governed, the final and capstone natural right is the right not to consent to any government. When the state assaults freedom and offers no accountability, are we simply to consider the matter as a lost cause? No! We must do just as the colonists did in 1776: alter or abolish the government and institute a new system of laws that allows us to pursue our natural yearnings.

On the concept of a social compact. To be specific, since the federal government came about by the states freely ceding limited powers to it, why can't the states take back those powers? If I can no longer consent to the government that lies, cheats, steals, and kills in my name, why cannot I simply withhold my consent and ignore it? If the government exists only because free persons have freely given some of their natural freedoms to it, if the sole moral underpinning of the government in America is the free consent of the governed, what becomes of the government when that consent is withdrawn?

What were Thomas Jefferson's views on our right to disobey the government?

Thomas Jefferson argued that once a government strays from its just powers, it is the right of the people to remove the government, by altering it, abolishing it, or, in the colonists' case, fighting a war for independence and then implementing a new and just government. When government becomes the enemy of Natural Rights, it can be tossed out. Rights are permanent, inherent features of all humans; governments are devices that can come and go according to the wishes of those who cede power to it. *Our Natural Rights cannot be changed or abolished; but governments can.*

Jefferson also pointed out that revolutions should not be started for trivial reasons, but only when governments become despotic or tyrannical. At the same time he issued a warning against complacency, because as he explained "[E]ternal vigilance is the price of liberty."[43] When a government engages in behavior designed to obscure or deliberately ignore your rights, and when the government's function is not to serve you but for you to serve it, you not only have a right to get rid of the government, but you have a positive moral duty to get rid of it. Put differently, "The tree of liberty must be refreshed from time to time with the blood of patriots and tyrants."[44]

Conclusion

What about our federal government today has put the US Constitution in exile?

The United States Constitution established the framework for a federal government holding only specific, enumerated powers, carefully and precisely delegated. Yet today the federal government recognizes no limitations on its power. The federal government does whatever it wants to do. It has actually involved itself, or threatened to do so, in a vast array of human behavior nowhere even hinted at in the Constitution.

In essence, the feds say: "Don't like the drinking age in South Dakota? We'll just threaten their highway funds, and they'll come around." Today the federal government intrudes itself into—among other things—the blood alcohol level of automobile drivers, the legal drinking age, the amount of wheat a farmer can grow for his own use, the ability of a terminally ill cancer patient to grow medical marijuana for personal use, the amount of sugar manufacturers can use in ketchup, steroids in athletes' blood, and the size of toilets in private homes.

The Founders gave us a small, discrete federal government, one of strictly limited powers; powers to address issues that are federal in nature. The Congress has confused *federal* with *national*, and has chosen to regulate any issue that it thinks affects more than one state.

— 216 —

What is the fundamental flaw in American political culture?

The fundamental flaw in our American political culture today is that we no longer believe that the government exists to serve our needs as individuals and members of a community. Instead, we seem to believe that the government is our master and therefore—since it is not bound by any constraints—able to determine for itself what is in our best interest.

Case in point. No one seriously believes that granting the government the ability to hack into our e-mail accounts—as the PATRIOT Act does—is truly in pursuit of American liberty. However, what people *do* believe is that there is nothing fundamentally illegal or unnatural or unconstitutional about granting government such a blank check. Although these policies may be "misguided," folks today believe they are not in violation of the Natural Law per se. When we hold such a view, we are one tenuous showing of necessity away from becoming complacent about illegitimate commands, as occurred with the Iraq War. Few Americans, for instance, seriously challenged the *lawfulness* of the war, but instead merely asked whether it was *militarily* necessary.

What is needed is not merely greater accountability, propriety, or guidance on Capitol Hill, but a seismic shift in the way Americans think about the constitutionally mandated role and contours of government. Anything less will accelerate our path to eventual serfdom.

Just as it was—in Thomas Paine's view—our positive moral duty to organize mass disobedience of unjust laws by spreading the message of independence, individual liberty, and natural rights, and thus to expose the unjust actions of the British government, it is our duty to spread this same message and expose the unjust actions of the current American government. Most importantly, we must engage in civil disobedience of those unjust laws.

Our right—our moral duty—to ignore or disobey an unjust government has been articulated by many powerful American thinkers throughout our history. As explained by Henry David Thoreau, if no action is taken by an individual to disobey and change an unjust law or legal system, that person practically becomes a supporter or an enabler of the unjust law or legal system, and anyone who supports an unjust law or legal system is acting in violation of the morality set forth by the Natural Law.

So I urge you to act. No longer shall Americans sit idly by at home and accept the status quo while injustice surrounds us. It is time to start peacefully fighting the injustice that takes place in our state legislatures as well as in

Washington, DC. The entire collapse of human liberty as outlined in this book has happened because states have enforced unjust laws for too long, and, instead of exercising their positive moral duty of civil disobedience, persons in those states have obeyed those unjust laws for too long. We must learn the lessons taught in Thomas Paine's *Common Sense*, demanded in the Declaration of Independence, and promised in the Bill of Rights, and we must stop obeying the unjust laws with which the government enslaves. No longer shall we sit idly by while the shackles of tyranny hold us down. We must stand up and fight. We must fight for our right to be free.

It is clear that the government has a free hand when it comes to prosecuting people for both genuine and government-created crimes, while disregarding the Constitution in the process. But let us not lose sight of the fact that we are still a free society, and, notwithstanding a huge, entrenched bureaucracy, those who set policy in the executive and legislative branches are still popularly elected.

Ultimately, the fate of American liberty is in the hands of American voters. Though we are less free with every tick of the clock, most of us still believe that the government is supposed to serve the people—fairly, not selectively.

There are some surprisingly direct ways to address the issues covered in this book.

Apply the Law to Everyone

First, Congress and the state legislatures should enact legislation simply requiring that the police and all law enforcement personnel, and everyone who works for or is an agent of the government, be governed by, subject to, and required to comply with all the laws.

This, of course, would render useless arguments like "the bribery statute doesn't apply to the government." This would also prevent police officers from walking through Washington Square Park and attempting to sell drugs in the presence of children. This would eliminate virtually all entrapment, and it would enhance respect for the law. How many times have you seen a police officer turn on a siren to go through a red light or park in front of a fire hydrant or drive the wrong way down a one-way street for no apparent reason (perhaps, to invoke a cynical stereotype, just to get donuts and coffee)?

Theoretically, if the police are required to obey the same laws as the rest of us, our respect for them and for the laws they enforce would dramatically increase, and their jobs would become easier. This would also mean that no person could be prosecuted for any crime if, during the lead-up to the prosecution, the police committed a crime. In short, it would be against the law to break the law. It may seem silly to suggest that the government adopt a law stating that the government must follow the law, but the many instances of government law-breaking and abuse demonstrates that such a law enforcing the law is necessary.

Congress and the state legislatures should also make it easier to sue the federal and state governments for monetary damages when they violate our constitutional liberties.

The federal government and many states have rendered themselves immune (called "sovereign immunity") from such lawsuits if the lawsuit attacks the exercise of discretion by government employees. This is nonsense. You can sue your neighbor for negligence if his car runs over your garden or your dog. You can sue a corporation if it pollutes the air you breathe. You can sue your physician if he leaves a scalpel in your belly.

You should be able to sue the local police, state police, and the FBI under the same legal theories if they torment you, if they prevent you from speaking freely, if they bribe witnesses to testify against you, if they steal your property, or if they break the law in order to convict you.

Along with removing sovereign immunity, I would also remove personal immunity on the part of individuals who work for the government when they commit crimes. Let me explain what I mean.

If a corporation harms you by selling you a defective product, you may sue the individuals who work for the corporation who actually caused the defect, as well as the corporation itself. The individuals are usually indemnified, that is, their legal bills are paid and any settlements or judgments against them are paid by the corporation that employs them. If they have committed a crime during the course of their employment that led to the defect, their employer cannot indemnify them, and they are personally exposed to your lawsuit. The same should be the case for government employees and agents. If a government employee commits a crime in the course of his work, he should lose all immunity and be exposed personally to litigation by the victim of the crime. This would be a strong and cost-effective way to compel the government, its employees, and agents to obey the same laws they are sworn to enforce.

In some states and in the federal system, if a litigant files a frivolous pleading with the Court or makes an indefensible argument to the Court, the litigant must pay the legal fees of his adversary for resisting the pleading or the argument. This rule should be applied as well to the federal and state governments in civil and in criminal cases. If a defendant is ultimately exonerated in a criminal case, and the government broke the law to prosecute him, the government should pay his legal bills.

Defend the Constitution

My political friends have often attacked the concept of "judicial activism." By this they mean they strongly condemn a judge's substitution of his or her judgments for that of the legislature or the executive. Let's be brutally honest about this: The only judicial activism we condemn is that with which we disagree. One man's judicial activism is another man's heroic defense of the Constitution. When judicial activism merely enforces the Constitution, it is a very good concept.

If, for example, a state legislature were to enact a statute authorizing the enslavement of household domestic help, a judge would surely strike the statute down as being in violation of the Thirteenth Amendment. Would anyone call that judicial activism?

If Congress were to enact a statute making it a criminal offense to criticize the Congress, and a judge were to invalidate the statute as being in violation of the First Amendment, would anyone call that judicial activism?

The answers to these questions are clear because the violations of the Constitution are clear. Judges are attacked for being judicial activists only by those who disagree with the judges' decisions. In my two hypotheticals there would be some people who would attack the acts of these judges as judicial activism: those who wanted to possess slaves and incumbent members of Congress.

On the other side of judicial activism is judicial tyranny. If, for example, a teachers' union thinks a city should budget more money for its teachers' salaries, and the mayor says no, and the union sues and gets a judge to agree, and the judge orders the city to pay higher salaries, that judicial act is tyrannical. Why? It is within the institutional function of the judiciary to say what the Constitution means; it is not within the judicial function—its competence—to raise taxes, fix salaries, or set a budget. Those functions are expressly given by law to the other two branches of government. Judges should only invalidate the acts of Congress or the president in cases of clear contradiction of the Constitution and when natural rights have been impaired.

Please do not forget that the American system of government is not a democracy, it is a republic; and it has features that are distinctly antidemocratic. To paraphrase Professor

Laurence Tribe of Harvard Law School, the whole reason we have an independent, life-tenured federal judiciary is to put brakes on democracy, to prevent the tyranny of the majority. Without a judiciary checking the behavior of Congress and the president—making certain they conform to the Constitution—nothing could prevent the majority from taking property or freedom from those it despised.

Check Government Crimes

One of the ultimate lessons of this book is that for the government, crime pays. It makes prosecution easier and virtually guarantees success.

When a person or corporation breaks the law, they are prosecuted and, if convicted, they are punished. Theoretically, the punishment makes society whole, as best we can do in a free society. We don't any longer believe in an eye for an eye or a tooth for a tooth. We somehow accept the idea that a robber who steals ten thousand dollars from a bank and, after conviction, is forced to return it and serve ten years in jail, has wiped his slate clean; and that a polluter who has harmed the waters or the air, but has been made to pay the cost of cleaning up the pollution and serve jail time, has also wiped the slate clean.

But when the government commits a crime, and the offending government actors are not prosecuted, it becomes a *precedent*; no slate is wiped clean.

Worse, the precedent becomes a basis for the same government and other governments to do likewise in the future. The precedent breeds disrespect and frustration. The precedent tramples human liberties, and it makes those who run the government, however brief their tenure, close to tyrants. The precedent is contagious because unpunished crime is contagious; it breeds contempt for law and invites some to become a law unto themselves.

If the Constitution is enforced selectively, according to the contemporary wants and needs of the government, we will continue to see free speech suppressed on inexplicable whims; police targeting the weak and killing the innocent; government lying to its citizens, stealing their property, tricking them into criminal acts, bribing its witnesses against them, making a mockery of legal reasoning, and breaking the laws in order to enforce them. A government that commits crime is not your friend.

This is not the type of government we, the people, have authorized to exist, and it is not the type of government that we should tolerate. We can do better. If government crimes are not checked, our Constitution will be meaningless, and our attempts to understand and enforce and rely on it will be chaotic.

In what ways should the Constitution be amended so that big government can be kept in better check?

We have the power to build our government anew. The states—remember them? they created the federal government—have the power to force Congress to hold a constitutional convention to clarify just a few words in the document, so as to keep the government in check.

1. "We the People" in the preamble should be made historically accurate so as to read, "We the States."
2. Article VIII which grants Congress the power "to regulate Commerce among the several States," should be amended so as to read, "To keep commerce regular . . . among the several States."
3. The Tenth Amendment should have reinserted back into it the word *expressly*, so that it will read: "The powers not expressly delegated to the United States by the Constitution, nor prohibited by it to the States, are reserved to the States respectively, or to the people."
4. The Sixteenth Amendment, which authorizes Congress to tax personal incomes, should be abolished outright.

It is the constant stream of money from this source that has corrupted every tax-and-spend Congress for the past ninety years.

5. The Seventeenth Amendment, which provides for the popular election of senators, should be abolished. This would return their election to state legislatures and thus would guarantee representation of the states as sovereign entities in the federal government. The more sovereign the states are, the more independent will be their laws, thus ensuring more choices to Americans. Ronald Reagan loved this concept, and said it enabled us "to vote with our feet," by moving to a state whose laws we prefer. Choice equals freedom.

6. If any lesson is clear from this history, it is that the federal government will never check its own power. On the contrary, it will continue to take liberty and thus property whenever and from whomsoever it wishes. Thus, I would clarify the right of the states to secede from the Union, losing all the benefits that come from membership, but regaining all the freedom membership has taken away. This is not as drastic as it sounds. The United States has had territories and commonwealths for over one hundred years. Many enjoy great prosperity and quiescence without a federal boot on their throats. And their residents do not pay a federal income tax.

The government's sole moral obligation is to preserve freedom. And freedom is the unfettered ability to choose to follow your own conscience and free will, not the will of someone in the government. If the government keeps us safe but not free, the government will have become tyrannical, and it will be as illegitimate as was the government of King George III in 1776. And it will be time for the government to go.

It has been 240 years since last we dispatched tyranny from America. Is the spirit that animated the Founders in 1776 still alive? Are there those among us who unambiguously declare that liberty trumps safety? Is life so sweet and peace so dear that we would prefer to live as slaves rather than risk perishing for freedom?

Sadly, since the day of its ratification, our Constitution has been battered and worn down to its very bones, leaving our liberty a mere skeleton of what our Founders intended. But all the injustice in the world can never destroy the hope of restoring freedom, just as all the darkness in the world can never extinguish the flame in our hearts.

The Founders' dream lives in each and every human being, as does the power to turn it into a reality. Although it is dangerous to be right when the government is wrong, that danger is nothing compared to the danger of languishing for the remainder of our lives under the physical and spiritual chains of tyrants.

What charge do you have for your readers
before they close this book?

Ronald Reagan reminded us many times that we have the power to begin the world anew. I agree—and we should start with a government faithful to the Constitution, one whose mantra is freedom, not safety; one that acknowledges that the government is the servant, not the master.

The Constitution was not written in order to right every wrong. It was not written to allow every federal do-gooder and busybody to impose his notion of clean living, safe working, or pure thinking on individuals. It was written to keep governmental power diffused, to restrain the government from interfering with the Natural Law, toward one solitary goal: the freedom of the individual to pursue happiness.

Do we still have a Constitution? Dear readers, you can make that call. I say it has been sent into exile, and we must reclaim it before it is too late.

The Constitution of the United States

We the People of the United States, in Order to form a more perfect Union, establish Justice, insure domestic Tranquility, provide for the common defense, promote the general Welfare, and secure the Blessings of Liberty to ourselves and our Posterity, do ordain and establish this Constitution for the United States of America.

Article 1

Section 1. All legislative Powers herein granted shall be vested in a Congress of the United States, which shall consist of a Senate and House of Representatives.

Section 2. The House of Representatives shall be composed of Members chosen every second Year by the People of the several States, and the Electors in each State shall have the Qualifications requisite for Electors of the most numerous Branch of the State Legislature.

No Person shall be a Representative who shall not have attained to the Age of twenty five Years, and been seven Years a Citizen of the United States, and who shall not, when elected, be an Inhabitant of that State in which he shall be chosen.

Representatives and direct Taxes shall be apportioned among the several States which may be included within this Union, according to their respective Numbers, which shall be determined by adding to the whole Number of free Persons, including those bound to Service for a Term of Years, and excluding Indians not taxed, three fifths of all other Persons.[1] The actual Enumeration shall be made within three Years after the first Meeting of the Congress of the United States, and within every subsequent Term of ten Years, in such Manner as they shall by Law direct. The Number of Representatives shall not exceed one for every thirty Thousand, but each State shall have at Least one Representative; and until such enumeration shall be made, the State of New Hampshire shall be entitled to choose three, Massachusetts eight, Rhode-Island and Providence Plantations one, Connecticut five, New-York six, New Jersey four, Pennsylvania eight, Delaware one, Maryland six, Virginia ten, North Carolina five, South Carolina five, and Georgia three.

When vacancies happen in the Representation from any State, the Executive Authority thereof shall issue Writs of Election to fill such Vacancies.

The House of Representatives shall choose their Speaker and other Officers; and shall have the sole Power of Impeachment.

Section 3. The Senate of the United States shall be composed of two Senators from each State, chosen by the Legislature[2] thereof for six Years; and each Senator shall have one Vote.

Immediately after they shall be assembled in Consequence of the first Election, they shall be divided as equally as may be into three Classes. The Seats of the Senators of the first Class shall be vacated at the Expiration of the second Year, of the second Class at the Expiration of the fourth Year, and of the third Class at the Expiration of the sixth Year, so that one third may be chosen every second Year; and if Vacancies happen by Resignation, or otherwise, during the Recess of the Legislature of any State, the Executive thereof may make temporary Appointments until the next Meeting of the Legislature, which shall then fill such Vacancies.[3]

No Person shall be a Senator who shall not have attained to the Age of thirty Years, and been nine Years a Citizen of the United States, and who shall not, when elected, be an Inhabitant of that State for which he shall be chosen.

The Vice President of the United States shall be President of the Senate, but shall have no Vote, unless they be equally divided.

The Senate shall choose their other Officers, and also a President pro tempore, in the Absence of the Vice President, or when he shall exercise the Office of President of the United States.

The Senate shall have the sole Power to try all Impeachments. When sitting for that Purpose, they shall be on Oath or Affirmation. When the President of the United States is tried, the Chief Justice shall preside: And no Person shall be convicted without the Concurrence of two thirds of the Members present.

Judgment in Cases of Impeachment shall not extend further than to removal from Office, and disqualification to hold and enjoy any Office of honor, Trust or Profit under the United States: but the Party convicted shall nevertheless be liable and subject to Indictment, Trial, Judgment and Punishment, according to Law.

Section 4. The Times, Places and Manner of holding Elections for Senators and Representatives, shall be prescribed in each State by the Legislature thereof; but the Congress may at any time by Law make or alter such Regulations, except as to the Places of choosing Senators.

The Congress shall assemble at least once in every Year, and such Meeting shall be on the first Monday in December,[4] unless they shall by Law appoint a different Day.

Section 5. Each House shall be the Judge of the Elections, Returns and Qualifications of its own Members, and a Majority of each shall constitute a Quorum to do Business; but a smaller Number may adjourn from day to day, and may be authorized to compel the Attendance of absent Members, in such Manner, and under such Penalties as each House may provide.

Each House may determine the Rules of its Proceedings, punish its Members for disorderly Behavior, and, with the Concurrence of two thirds, expel a Member.

Each House shall keep a Journal of its Proceedings, and from time to time publish the same, excepting such Parts as may in their Judgment require Secrecy; and the Yeas and Nays of the Members of either House on any question shall, at the Desire of one fifth of those Present, be entered on the Journal.

Neither House, during the Session of Congress, shall, without the Consent of the other, adjourn for more than three days, nor to any other Place than that in which the two Houses shall be sitting.

Section 6. The Senators and Representatives shall receive a Compensation for their Services, to be ascertained by Law, and paid out of the Treasury of the United States. They shall in all Cases, except Treason, Felony and Breach of the Peace, be privileged from Arrest during their Attendance at the Session of their respective Houses, and in going to and returning from the same; and for any Speech or Debate in either House, they shall not be questioned in any other Place.

No Senator or Representative shall, during the Time for which he was elected, be appointed to any civil Office under the Authority of the United States, which shall have been created, or the Emoluments whereof shall have been increased during such time; and no Person holding any Office under the United States, shall be a Member of either House during his Continuance in Office.

Section 7. All Bills for raising Revenue shall originate in the House of Representatives; but the Senate may propose or concur with Amendments as on other Bills.

Every Bill which shall have passed the House of Representatives and the Senate, shall, before it become a Law, be presented to the President of the United States: If he approve he shall sign it, but if not he shall return it, with his Objections to that House in which it shall have originated, who shall enter the Objections at large on their Journal, and proceed to reconsider it. If after such Reconsideration two thirds of that House shall agree to pass the Bill, it shall be sent, together with the Objections, to the other House, by which it shall likewise be reconsidered, and if approved by two thirds of that House, it shall become a Law. But in all such Cases the Votes of both Houses shall be determined by yeas and Nays, and the Names of the Persons voting for and against the Bill shall be entered on the Journal of each House respectively. If any Bill shall not be returned by the President within ten Days (Sundays excepted) after it shall have been presented to him, the Same shall be a Law, in like Manner as if he had signed it, unless the Congress by their Adjournment prevent its Return, in which Case it shall not be a Law.

Every Order, Resolution, or Vote to which the Concurrence of the Senate and House of Representatives may be necessary (except on a question of Adjournment) shall be presented to the President of the United States; and before the Same shall take Effect, shall be approved by him, or being disapproved by him, shall be repassed by two thirds of the Senate and House of Representatives, according to the Rules and Limitations prescribed in the Case of a Bill.

Section 8. The Congress shall have Power To lay and collect Taxes, Duties, Imposts and Excises, to pay the Debts and provide for the common Defense and general Welfare of the United States; but all Duties, Imposts and Excises shall be uniform throughout the United States;

To borrow Money on the credit of the United States;

To regulate Commerce with foreign Nations, and among the several States, and with the Indian Tribes;

To establish an uniform Rule of Naturalization, and uniform Laws on the subject of Bankruptcies throughout the United States;

To coin Money, regulate the Value thereof, and of foreign Coin, and fix the Standard of Weights and Measures;

To provide for the Punishment of counterfeiting the Securities and current Coin of the United States;

To establish Post Offices and post Roads;

To promote the Progress of Science and useful Arts, by securing for limited Times to Authors and Inventors the exclusive Right to their respective Writings and Discoveries;

To constitute Tribunals inferior to the supreme Court;

To define and punish Piracies and Felonies committed on the high Seas, and Offences against the Law of Nations;

To declare War, grant Letters of Marque and Reprisal, and make Rules concerning Captures on Land and Water;

To raise and support Armies, but no Appropriation of Money to that Use shall be for a longer Term than two Years;

To provide and maintain a Navy;

To make Rules for the Government and Regulation of the land and naval Forces;

To provide for calling forth the Militia to execute the Laws of the Union, suppress Insurrections and repel Invasions;

To provide for organizing, arming, and disciplining the Militia, and for governing such Part of them as may be employed in the Service of the United States, reserving to the States respectively, the Appointment of the Officers, and the Authority of training the Militia according to the discipline prescribed by Congress;

To exercise exclusive Legislation in all Cases whatsoever, over such District (not exceeding ten Miles square) as may, by Cession of particular States, and the Acceptance of Congress, become the Seat of the Government of the United States, and to exercise like Authority over all Places purchased by the Consent of the Legislature of the State in which the Same shall be, for the Erection of Forts, Magazines, Arsenals, dock-Yards, and other needful Buildings;—And

To make all Laws which shall be necessary and proper for carrying into Execution the foregoing Powers, and all other

Powers vested by this Constitution in the Government of the United States, or in any Department or Officer thereof.

Section 9. The Migration or Importation of such Persons as any of the States now existing shall think proper to admit, shall not be prohibited by the Congress prior to the Year one thousand eight hundred and eight, but a Tax or duty may be imposed on such Importation, not exceeding ten dollars for each Person.

The Privilege of the Writ of Habeas Corpus shall not be suspended, unless when in Cases of Rebellion or Invasion the public Safety may require it.

No Bill of Attainder or ex post facto Law shall be passed.

No Capitation, or other direct, Tax shall be laid, unless in Proportion to the Census or enumeration herein before directed to be taken.[5]

No Tax or Duty shall be laid on Articles exported from any State.

No Preference shall be given by any Regulation of Commerce or Revenue to the Ports of one State over those of another; nor shall Vessels bound to, or from, one State, be obliged to enter, clear, or pay Duties in another.

No Money shall be drawn from the Treasury, but in Consequence of Appropriations made by Law; and a regular Statement and Account of the Receipts and Expenditures of all public Money shall be published from time to time.

No Title of Nobility shall be granted by the United States. And no Person holding any Office of Profit or Trust under them, shall, without the Consent of the Congress, accept of any present, Emolument, Office, or Title, of any kind whatever, from any King, Prince, or foreign State.

Section 10. No State shall enter into any Treaty, Alliance, or Confederation; grant Letters of Marque and Reprisal; coin Money; emit Bills of Credit; make any Thing but gold and silver Coin a Tender in Payment of Debts; pass any Bill of Attainder, ex post facto Law, or Law impairing the Obligation of Contracts, or grant any Title of Nobility.

No State shall, without the Consent of the Congress, lay any Imposts or Duties on Imports or Exports, except what may be absolutely necessary for executing its inspection Laws: and the net Produce of all Duties and Imposts, laid by any State on Imports or Exports, shall be for the Use of the Treasury of the United States; and all such Laws shall be subject to the Revision and Control of the Congress.

No State shall, without the Consent of Congress, lay any Duty of Tonnage, keep Troops, or Ships of War in time of Peace, enter into any Agreement or Compact with another State, or with a foreign Power, or engage in War, unless actually invaded, or in such imminent Danger as will not admit of delay.

Article 2

Section 1. The executive Power shall be vested in a President of the United States of America. He shall hold his Office during the Term of four Years, and, together with the Vice President, chosen for the same Term, be elected, as follows:

Each State shall appoint, in such Manner as the Legislature thereof may direct, a Number of Electors, equal to the whole Number of Senators and Representatives to which the State may be entitled in the Congress: but no Senator or Representative, or Person holding an Office of Trust or Profit under the United States, shall be appointed an Elector.

The Electors shall meet in their respective States, and vote by Ballot for two Persons, of whom one at least shall not be an Inhabitant of the same State with themselves. And they shall make a List of all the Persons voted for, and of the Number of Votes for each; which List they shall sign and certify, and transmit sealed to the Seat of the Government of the United States, directed to the President of the Senate. The President of the Senate shall, in the Presence of the Senate and House of Representatives, open all the Certificates, and the Votes shall then be counted. The Person having the greatest Number of Votes shall be the President, if such Number be a Majority of the whole Number of Electors appointed; and if there be more than one who have such Majority, and have an equal Number of Votes, then the House of Representatives shall immediately choose by Ballot one of them for President; and if no Person have a Majority, then from the five highest on the List the said House shall in like Manner choose the President. But in choosing the President, the Votes shall be taken by States, the Representation from each State having one Vote; A quorum for this purpose shall consist of a Member or Members from two thirds of the States, and a Majority of all the States shall be necessary to a Choice. In every Case, after the Choice of the President, the Person having the greatest Number of Votes of the Electors shall be the Vice President. But if there should remain two or more who have equal Votes, the Senate shall choose from them by Ballot the Vice President.[6]

The Congress may determine the Time of choosing the Electors, and the Day on which they shall give their Votes; which Day shall be the same throughout the United States.

No Person except a natural born Citizen, or a Citizen of the United States, at the time of the Adoption of this Constitution, shall be eligible to the Office of President; neither shall any Person be eligible to that Office who shall not have attained to the Age of thirty five Years, and been fourteen Years a Resident within the United States.

In Case of the Removal of the President from Office, or of his Death, Resignation, or Inability to discharge the Powers and Duties of the said Office, the Same shall devolve on the Vice President, and the Congress may by Law provide for the Case of Removal, Death, Resignation or Inability, both of the President and Vice President, declaring what Officer shall then act as President, and such Officer shall act accordingly, until the Disability be removed, or a President shall be elected.[7]

The President shall, at stated Times, receive for his Services, a Compensation, which shall neither be increased nor diminished during the Period for which he shall have been elected, and he shall not receive within that Period any other Emolument from the United States, or any of them.

Before he enters on the Execution of his Office, he shall take the following Oath or Affirmation:—"I do solemnly swear (or affirm) that I will faithfully execute the Office of President of the United States, and will to the best of my Ability, preserve, protect and defend the Constitution of the United States."

Section 2. The President shall be Commander in Chief of the Army and Navy of the United States, and of the Militia of the several States, when called into the actual Service of the United States; he may require the Opinion, in writing, of the principal Officer in each of the executive Departments, upon any Subject relating to the Duties of their respective Offices, and he shall have Power to grant Reprieves and Pardons for Offences against the United States, except in Cases of Impeachment.

He shall have Power, by and with the Advice and Consent of the Senate, to make Treaties, provided two thirds of the Senators present concur; and he shall nominate, and by and with the Advice and Consent of the Senate, shall appoint Ambassadors, other public Ministers and Consuls, Judges of the supreme Court, and all other Officers of the United States, whose Appointments are not herein otherwise provided for, and which shall be established by Law: but the Congress may by Law vest the Appointment of such inferior Officers, as they think proper, in the President alone, in the Courts of Law, or in the Heads of Departments.

The President shall have Power to fill up all Vacancies that may happen during the Recess of the Senate, by granting Commissions which shall expire at the End of their next Session.

Section 3. He shall from time to time give to the Congress Information of the State of the Union, and recommend to their Consideration such Measures as he shall judge necessary and expedient; he may, on extraordinary Occasions, convene both Houses, or either of them, and in Case of Disagreement between them, with Respect to the Time of Adjournment, he may adjourn them to such Time as he shall think proper; he shall receive Ambassadors and other public Ministers; he shall take Care that the Laws be faithfully executed, and shall Commission all the Officers of the United States.

Section 4. The President, Vice President and all civil Officers of the United States, shall be removed from Office on Impeachment for, and Conviction of, Treason, Bribery, or other high Crimes and Misdemeanors.

Article 3

Section 1. The judicial Power of the United States shall be vested in one supreme Court, and in such inferior Courts as the Congress may from time to time ordain and establish. The Judges, both of the supreme and inferior Courts, shall hold their Offices during good Behavior, and shall, at stated Times, receive for their Services a Compensation, which shall not be diminished during their Continuance in Office.

Section 2. The judicial Power shall extend to all Cases, in Law and Equity, arising under this Constitution, the Laws of the United States, and Treaties made, or which shall be made, under their Authority;—to all Cases affecting Ambassadors, other public Ministers and Consuls;—to all Cases of admiralty and maritime Jurisdiction;—to Controversies to which the United States shall be a Party;—to Controversies between two or more States;—between a State and Citizens of another State[8];—between Citizens of different States;—between Citizens of the same State claiming Lands under Grants of different States, and between a State, or the Citizens thereof, and foreign States, Citizens or Subjects.

In all Cases affecting Ambassadors, other public Ministers and Consuls, and those in which a State shall be Party, the supreme Court shall have original Jurisdiction. In all the other Cases before mentioned, the supreme Court shall have appellate Jurisdiction, both as to Law and Fact, with such Exceptions, and under such Regulations as the Congress shall make.

The Trial of all Crimes, except in Cases of Impeachment, shall be by Jury; and such Trial shall be held in the State where the said Crimes shall have been committed; but when not committed within any State, the Trial shall be at such Place or Places as the Congress may by Law have directed.

Section 3. Treason against the United States, shall consist only in levying War against them, or in adhering to their Enemies, giving them Aid and Comfort. No Person shall be convicted of Treason unless on the Testimony of two Witnesses to the same overt Act, or on Confession in open Court.

The Congress shall have Power to declare the Punishment of Treason, but no Attainder of Treason shall work Corruption of Blood, or Forfeiture except during the Life of the Person attainted.

Article 4

Section 1. Full Faith and Credit shall be given in each State to the public Acts, Records, and judicial Proceedings of every other State. And the Congress may by general Laws prescribe the Manner in which such Acts, Records and Proceedings shall be proved, and the Effect thereof.

Section 2. The Citizens of each State shall be entitled to all Privileges and Immunities of Citizens in the several States.

A Person charged in any State with Treason, Felony, or other Crime, who shall flee from Justice, and be found in another State, shall on Demand of the executive Authority of the State from which he fled, be delivered up, to be removed to the State having Jurisdiction of the Crime.

No Person held to Service or Labor in one State, under the Laws thereof, escaping into another, shall, in Consequence of any Law or Regulation therein, be discharged from such Service or Labor, but shall be delivered up on Claim of the Party to whom such Service or Labor may be due.[9]

Section 3. New States may be admitted by the Congress into this Union; but no new State shall be formed or erected within the Jurisdiction of any other State; nor any State be formed by the Junction of two or more States, or Parts of States, without the Consent of the Legislatures of the States concerned as well as of the Congress.

The Congress shall have Power to dispose of and make all needful Rules and Regulations respecting the Territory or other Property belonging to the United States; and nothing in this Constitution shall be so construed as to Prejudice any Claims of the United States, or of any particular State.

Section 4. The United States shall guarantee to every State in this Union a Republican Form of Government, and shall protect each of them against Invasion; and on Application of the Legislature, or of the Executive (when the Legislature cannot be convened), against domestic Violence.

Article 5

The Congress, whenever two thirds of both Houses shall deem it necessary, shall propose Amendments to this

Constitution, or, on the Application of the Legislatures of two thirds of the several States, shall call a Convention for proposing Amendments, which, in either Case, shall be valid to all Intents and Purposes, as Part of this Constitution, when ratified by the Legislatures of three fourths of the several States, or by Conventions in three fourths thereof, as the one or the other Mode of Ratification may be proposed by the Congress; Provided that no Amendment which may be made prior to the Year One thousand eight hundred and eight shall in any Manner affect the first and fourth Clauses in the Ninth Section of the first Article; and that no State, without its Consent, shall be deprived of its equal Suffrage in the Senate.

Article 6

All Debts contracted and Engagements entered into, before the Adoption of this Constitution, shall be as valid against the United States under this Constitution, as under the Confederation.

This Constitution, and the Laws of the United States which shall be made in Pursuance thereof; and all Treaties made, or which shall be made, under the Authority of the United States, shall be the supreme Law of the Land; and the Judges in every State shall be bound thereby, any Thing in the Constitution or Laws of any State to the Contrary notwithstanding.

The Senators and Representatives before mentioned, and the Members of the several State Legislatures, and all executive and judicial Officers, both of the United States and of the several States, shall be bound by Oath or Affirmation, to support this Constitution; but no religious Test shall ever be required as a Qualification to any Office or public Trust under the United States.

Article 7

The Ratification of the Conventions of nine States, shall be sufficient for the Establishment of this Constitution between the States so ratifying the Same.

The Word, "the," being interlined between the seventh and eighth Lines of the first Page, the Word "Thirty" being partly written on an Erasure in the fifteenth Line of the first Page, The Words "is tried" being interlined between the thirty second and thirty third Lines of the first Page and the Word "the" being interlined between the forty third and forty fourth Lines of the second Page.

Attest William Jackson Secretary

Done in Convention by the Unanimous Consent of the States present the Seventeenth Day of September in the Year of our Lord one thousand seven hundred and Eighty seven and of the Independence of the United States of

America the Twelfth In witness whereof We have hereunto subscribed our Names,

G. Washington
Presidt and deputy from Virginia

John Langdon
Nicholas Gilman

DELAWARE
Geo: Read
Gunning Bedford jun John Dickinson
Richard Bassett Jaco: Broom

MASSACHUSETTS
Nathaniel Gorham
Rufus King

MARYLAND
James McHenry
Dan of St Thos. Jenifer
Danl. Carroll

CONNECTICUT
Wm. Saml. Johnson
Roger Sherman

VIRGINIA
John Blair
James Madison Jr.

NEW YORK
Alexander Hamilton

NORTH CAROLINA
Wm. Blount
Richd. Dobbs Spaight
Hu Williamson

NEW JERSEY
Wil: Livingston
David Brearley
Wm. Paterson
Jona: Dayton

SOUTH CAROLINA
J. Rutledge
Charles Cotesworth Pinckney
Charles Pinckney
Pierce Butler

B Franklin
Thomas Mifflin
Robt. Morris
Geo. Clymer
Thos. FitzSimons
Jared Ingersoll
James Wilson
Gouv Morris

GEORGIA
William Few
Abr Baldwin

— 252 —

Articles of Amendment

Amendment 1

Congress shall make no law respecting an establishment of religion, or prohibiting the free exercise thereof; or abridging the freedom of speech, or of the press; or the right of the people peaceably to assemble, and to petition the Government for a redress of grievances.

Amendment 2

A well regulated Militia, being necessary to the security of a free State, the right of the people to keep and bear Arms, shall not be infringed.

Amendment 3

No Soldier shall, in time of peace be quartered in any house, without the consent of the Owner, nor in time of war, but in a manner to be prescribed by law.

Amendment 4

The right of the people to be secure in their persons, houses, papers, and effects, against unreasonable searches and seizures, shall not be violated, and no Warrants shall issue, but upon probable cause, supported by Oath or affirmation, and particularly describing the place to be searched, and the persons or things to be seized.

Amendment 5

No person shall be held to answer for a capital, or otherwise infamous crime, unless on a presentment or indictment of a Grand Jury, except in cases arising in the land or naval forces, or in the Militia, when in actual service in time of War or public danger; nor shall any person be subject for the same offense to be twice put in jeopardy of life or limb; nor shall be compelled in any criminal case to be a witness against himself, nor be deprived of life, liberty, or property, without due process of law; nor shall private property be taken for public use, without just compensation.

Amendment 6

In all criminal prosecutions, the accused shall enjoy the right to a speedy and public trial, by an impartial jury of the State and district wherein the crime shall have been committed, which district shall have been previously ascertained by law, and to be informed of the nature and cause of the accusation; to be confronted with the witnesses against him; to have compulsory process for obtaining witnesses in his favor, and to have the Assistance of Counsel for his defense.

Amendment 7

In Suits at common law, where the value in controversy shall exceed twenty dollars, the right of trial by jury shall be preserved, and no fact tried by a jury, shall be otherwise re-examined in any Court of the United States, than according to the rules of the common law.

Amendment 8

Excessive bail shall not be required, nor excessive fines imposed, nor cruel and unusual punishments inflicted.

Amendment 9

The enumeration in the Constitution, of certain rights, shall not be construed to deny or disparage others retained by the people.

Amendment 10

The powers not delegated to the United States by the Constitution, nor prohibited by it to the States, are reserved to the States respectively, or to the people.

Amendment 11

The Judicial power of the United States shall not be construed to extend to any suit in law or equity, commenced or prosecuted against one of the United States by Citizens of another State, or by Citizens or Subjects of any Foreign State.

Amendment 12

The Electors shall meet in their respective states and vote by ballot for President and Vice-President, one of whom, at least, shall not be an inhabitant of the same state with themselves; they shall name in their ballots the person voted for as President, and in distinct ballots the person voted for as Vice-President, and they shall make distinct lists of all persons voted for as President, and of all persons voted for as Vice-President, and of the number of votes for each, which lists they shall sign and certify, and transmit sealed to the seat of the government of the United States, directed to the President of the Senate;—the President of the Senate shall, in the presence of the Senate and House of Representatives, open all the certificates and the votes shall then be counted;—The person having the greatest number of votes for President, shall be the President, if such number be a majority of the whole number of Electors appointed; and if no person have such majority, then from the persons having the highest numbers not exceeding three on the list of those voted for as President, the House of Representatives shall choose immediately, by ballot, the President. But in choosing the President, the votes shall be taken by states, the representation from each state having one vote; a quorum for this purpose shall consist of a member or members from two-thirds of the states, and a majority of all the states shall be necessary to a choice. And if the House of Representatives shall not choose a President whenever the right of choice shall devolve upon them, before the fourth day of March next following, then the Vice-President shall act as President, as in case of the death or other constitutional disability of the President.—[10] The person having the greatest number of votes as Vice-President, shall be the Vice-President, if such number be a majority of the whole number of Electors appointed, and if no person have a majority, then from the two highest numbers on the list, the Senate shall choose the Vice-President; a quorum for the purpose shall consist of two-thirds of the whole number of Senators, and a majority of the whole number shall be necessary to a choice. But no person constitutionally ineligible to the office of President shall be eligible to that of Vice-President of the United States.

Amendment 13

Section 1. Neither slavery nor involuntary servitude, except as a punishment for crime whereof the party shall have been duly convicted, shall exist within the United States, or any place subject to their jurisdiction.

Section 2. Congress shall have power to enforce this article by appropriate legislation.

Amendment 14

Section 1. All persons born or naturalized in the United States, and subject to the jurisdiction thereof, are citizens of the United States and of the State wherein they reside. No State shall make or enforce any law which shall abridge the privileges or immunities of citizens of the United States; nor shall any State deprive any person of life, liberty, or property, without due process of law; nor deny to any person within its jurisdiction the equal protection of the laws.

Section 2. Representatives shall be apportioned among the several States according to their respective numbers, counting the whole number of persons in each State, excluding Indians not taxed. But when the right to vote at any election for the choice of electors for President and Vice-President of the United States, Representatives in Congress, the Executive and Judicial officers of a State, or the members of the Legislature thereof, is denied to any of the male inhabitants of such State, being twenty-one years of age,[11] and citizens of the United States, or in any way abridged, except for participation in rebellion, or other crime, the basis of representation therein shall be reduced in the proportion which the number of such male citizens shall bear to the whole number of male citizens twenty-one years of age in such State.

Section 3. No person shall be a Senator or Representative in Congress, or elector of President and Vice-President, or hold any office, civil or military, under the United States, or under any State, who, having previously taken an oath, as a member of Congress, or as an officer of the United States, or as a member of any State legislature, or as an executive or judicial officer of any State, to support the Constitution of the United States, shall have engaged in insurrection or rebellion against the same, or given aid or comfort to the enemies thereof. But Congress may by a vote of two-thirds of each House, remove such disability.

Section 4. The validity of the public debt of the United States, authorized by law, including debts incurred for payment of pensions and bounties for services in suppressing insurrection or rebellion, shall not be questioned. But neither the United States nor any State shall assume or pay any debt or obligation incurred in aid of insurrection or rebellion against the United States, or any claim for the loss or emancipation of any slave; but all such debts, obligations and claims shall be held illegal and void.

Section 5. The Congress shall have the power to enforce, by appropriate legislation, the provisions of this article.

Amendment 15

Section 1. The right of citizens of the United States to vote shall not be denied or abridged by the United States or by any State on account of race, color, or previous condition of servitude—

Section 2. The Congress shall have the power to enforce this article by appropriate legislation.

Amendment 16

The Congress shall have power to lay and collect taxes on incomes, from whatever source derived, without apportionment among the several States, and without regard to any census or enumeration.

Amendment 17

The Senate of the United States shall be composed of two Senators from each State, elected by the people thereof, for six years; and each Senator shall have one vote. The electors in each State shall have the qualifications requisite for electors of the most numerous branch of the State legislatures.

When vacancies happen in the representation of any State in the Senate, the executive authority of such State shall issue writs of election to fill such vacancies: Provided, That the legislature of any State may empower the executive thereof to make temporary appointments until the people fill the vacancies by election as the legislature may direct.

This amendment shall not be so construed as to affect the election or term of any Senator chosen before it becomes valid as part of the Constitution.

Amendment 18

Section 1. After one year from the ratification of this article the manufacture, sale, or transportation of intoxicating liquors within, the importation thereof into, or the exportation thereof from the United States and all territory subject to the jurisdiction thereof for beverage purposes is hereby prohibited.

Section 2. The Congress and the several States shall have concurrent power to enforce this article by appropriate legislation.

Section 3. This article shall be inoperative unless it shall have been ratified as an amendment to the Constitution by the legislatures of the several States, as provided in the

Constitution, within seven years from the date of the submission hereof to the States by the Congress.[12]

Amendment 19

The right of citizens of the United States to vote shall not be denied or abridged by the United States or by any State on account of sex.

Congress shall have power to enforce this article by appropriate legislation.

Amendment 20

Section 1. The terms of the President and the Vice President shall end at noon on the 20th day of January, and the terms of Senators and Representatives at noon on the 3d day of January, of the years in which such terms would have ended if this article had not been ratified; and the terms of their successors shall then begin.

Section 2. The Congress shall assemble at least once in every year, and such meeting shall begin at noon on the 3d day of January, unless they shall by law appoint a different day.

Section 3. If, at the time fixed for the beginning of the term of the President, the President elect shall have died, the Vice President elect shall become President. If a President shall not have been chosen before the time fixed for the beginning of his term, or if the President elect shall have failed to qualify, then the Vice President elect shall act as President until a President shall have qualified; and the

Congress may by law provide for the case wherein neither a President elect nor a Vice President shall have qualified, declaring who shall then act as President, or the manner in which one who is to act shall be selected, and such person shall act accordingly until a President or Vice President shall have qualified.

Section 4. The Congress may by law provide for the case of the death of any of the persons from whom the House of Representatives may choose a President whenever the right of choice shall have devolved upon them, and for the case of the death of any of the persons from whom the Senate may choose a Vice President whenever the right of choice shall have devolved upon them.

Section 5. Sections 1 and 2 shall take effect on the 15th day of October following the ratification of this article.

Section 6. This article shall be inoperative unless it shall have been ratified as an amendment to the Constitution by the legislatures of three-fourths of the several States within seven years from the date of its submission.

Amendment 21

Section 1. The eighteenth article of amendment to the Constitution of the United States is hereby repealed.

Section 2. The transportation or importation into any State, Territory, or Possession of the United States for delivery or use therein of intoxicating liquors, in violation of the laws thereof, is hereby prohibited.

Section 3. This article shall be inoperative unless it shall have been ratified as an amendment to the Constitution by conventions in the several States, as provided in the Constitution, within seven years from the date of the submission hereof to the States by the Congress.

Amendment 22

Section 1. No person shall be elected to the office of the President more than twice, and no person who has held the office of President, or acted as President, for more than two years of a term to which some other person was elected President shall be elected to the office of President more than once. But this Article shall not apply to any person holding the office of President when this Article was proposed by Congress, and shall not prevent any person who may be holding the office of President, or acting as President, during the term within which this Article becomes operative from holding the office of President or acting as President during the remainder of such term.

Section 2. This article shall be inoperative unless it shall have been ratified as an amendment to the Constitution by the legislatures of three-fourths of the several States within seven years from the date of its submission to the States by the Congress.

Amendment 23

Section 1. The District constituting the seat of Government of the United States shall appoint in such manner as Congress may direct:

A number of electors of President and Vice President equal to the whole number of Senators and Representatives in Congress to which the District would be entitled if it were a State, but in no event more than the least populous State; they shall be in addition to those appointed by the States, but they shall be considered, for the purposes of the election of President and Vice President, to be electors appointed by a State; and they shall meet in the District and perform such duties as provided by the twelfth article of amendment.

Section 2. The Congress shall have power to enforce this article by appropriate legislation.

Amendment 24

Section 1. The right of citizens of the United States to vote in any primary or other election for President or Vice President, for electors for President or Vice President, or for Senator or Representative in Congress, shall not be denied or abridged by the United States or any State by reason of failure to pay poll tax or other tax.

Section 2. The Congress shall have power to enforce this article by appropriate legislation.

Amendment 25

Section 1. In case of the removal of the President from office or of his death or resignation, the Vice President shall become President.

Section 2. Whenever there is a vacancy in the office of the Vice President, the President shall nominate a Vice President who shall take office upon confirmation by a majority vote of both Houses of Congress.

Section 3. Whenever the President transmits to the President pro tempore of the Senate and the Speaker of the House of Representatives his written declaration that he is unable to discharge the powers and duties of his office, and until he transmits to them a written declaration to the contrary, such powers and duties shall be discharged by the Vice President as Acting President.

Section 4. Whenever the Vice President and a majority of either the principal officers of the executive departments or of such other body as Congress may by law provide, transmit to the President pro tempore of the Senate and the Speaker of the House of Representatives their written declaration that the President is unable to discharge the powers and duties of his office, the Vice President shall immediately assume the powers and duties of the office as Acting President.

Thereafter, when the President transmits to the President pro tempore of the Senate and the Speaker of the House of

Representatives his written declaration that no inability exists, he shall resume the powers and duties of his office unless the Vice President and a majority of either the principal officers of the executive department or of such other body as Congress may by law provide, transmit within four days to the President pro tempore of the Senate and the Speaker of the House of Representatives their written declaration that the President is unable to discharge the powers and duties of his office. Thereupon Congress shall decide the issue, assembling within forty-eight hours for that purpose if not in session. If the Congress, within twenty-one days after receipt of the latter written declaration, or, if Congress is not in session, within twenty-one days after Congress is required to assemble, determines by two-thirds vote of both Houses that the President is unable to discharge the powers and duties of his office, the Vice President shall continue to discharge the same as Acting President; otherwise, the President shall resume the powers and duties of his office.

Amendment 26

Section 1. The right of citizens of the United States, who are eighteen years of age or older, to vote shall not be denied or abridged by the United States or by any State on account of age.

Section 2. The Congress shall have power to enforce this article by appropriate legislation.

Amendment 27

No law, varying the compensation for the services of the Senators and Representatives, shall take effect, until an election of representatives shall have intervened.

Notes

1. Modified by the Fourteenth Amendment.
2. Modified by the Seventeenth Amendment.
3. Also modified by the Seventeenth Amendment.
4. Modified by the Twentieth Amendment; part of the Twelfth Amendment was also superseded by the Twentieth.
5. Modified by the Sixteenth Amendment.
6. Partially superseded by the Twelfth Amendment.
7. Affected by the Twenty-fifth Amendment.
8. Modified by the Eleventh Amendment.
9. Superseded by the Thirteenth Amendment.
10. Superseded by the Twentieth Amendment.
11. Modified by the Twenty-sixth Amendment.
12. The Eighteenth Amendment was repealed by the Twenty-first.

Endnotes

Chapter 3: The Declaration of Independence and Our Founding Fathers: How Far We've Strayed

1. This is my favorite line from all the Supreme Court opinions.
2. See *United States v. Darby*, argued in 1941. *Darby* was *Wickard's* predecessor.
3. Fireside Chat on Reorganization of the Judiciary, March 9, 1937, available at: http://www.hpol.org/fdr/chat/. FDR's "Fireside Chats" were a key way in which he strung along Americans into buying his Big Government solutions to the nation's plight. These chats are legendary.

Chapter 4: Rights and Freedoms That Are Being Violated

1. Tarso Ramos, Regulatory Takings and Private Property Rights, available at http://www.publiceye.org/eyes/privprop.html.
2. Walter Block, Rent Control, available at http://www.econlib.org/library/Enc/RentControl.html.
3. See *Gonzales v. Raich*, 03-1454 U.S. (2005).
4. Geoffrey R. Stone, et al., *The First Amendment*, 3rd ed., Walters Kluwer, (2008), 20.
5. Dan Ackman, The Case of the Fat Aerobics Instructor, May 9, 2002, available at http://www.forbes.com/2002/05/09/0509portnick.html.
6. George Getz, "Fat Law" Should Be Repealed, May 14, 2002, available at http://www.ifeminists.com/introduction/editorials/2002/0514b.html.
7. John Stossel, Freedom of Association. May 25, 2010, available at http://stossel.blogs.foxbusiness.com/2010/05/25/oreilly-tonight-freedom-of-association/.
8. Charles W. Baird, "On Freedom of Association: Why Doesn't Freedom of Association. Apply in Labor Markets?" *The Freeman: Ideas on Liberty* 52, no. 7 (July 7, 2002).
9. Ibid.
10. David R. Henderson, "Raising the Minimum Wage Will Discourage Migration? It Just Ain't So!" *The Freeman: Ideas on Liberty* 56, no. 9 (November 2006).
11. Steve Chapman, "Legalize Immigration: It's Time to Focus on Letting Illegal Immigrants In," *Reason*, May 31, 2010, http://reason.com/archives/2010/05/31/legalize-immigration.
12. Whalen v. Roe, 429 U.S. 589, 598–600 (1977).
13. Adapted from Andrew P. Napolitano, "Constitutional Law: Walking on Thin Constitutional Ice," http://www.lewrockwell.com.
14. Andrew P. Napolitano, "How Congress Has Assaulted Our Freedoms in the Patriot Act," Lewrockwell.com, December 15, 2006, www.lewrockwell.com/orig6/napolitano2.html.
15. Stephanie Coontz, "Taking Marriage Private," *New York Times*, November 26, 2007, www.nytimes.com/2007/11/26/opinion/26coontz.html.
16. Dr. Sally Satel, "The Waiting Game," American Enterprise Institute for Public Policy Research, June 26, 2006, www.aei.org/docLib/20060607_SatelQF.pdf.s
17. John Stossel, "End the Drug War," Creators.com, http://www.creators.com/opinion/john-stossel/end-the-drug-war.html.
18. For a historical overview of Kristallnacht and the 1938 pogroms please see the United States Holocaust Memorial Museum's exhibition, http://www.ushmm.org/museum/exhibit/online/kristallnacht/frame.htm.
19. Michael Berenbaum, "Kristallnacht," Encyclopaedia Britannica Online, http://www.britannica.com/eBchecked/topic/323626/Kristallnacht.
20. Kathy Chang, "Those Who Were There Remember Kristallnacht, Holocaust," Greater Media Newspapers, http://ws.gmnews.com/news/2009-12-16/front_page/006.html.
21. *Supra* note 18.
22. Robert Faurisson, "The Warsaw Ghetto 'Uprising': Jewish Insurrection or German Police Operation?" *Journal of Historical Review* 14, no. 2 (March 1994): 2–5.0.
23. James T. Areddy, "Staring Down the Barrel: The Rise of Guns in China," *Wall Street Journal*, October 14, 2008.
24. Information from the Stockholm International Peace Research Institute (SIPRI), http:// www.sipri.org/. Please see the databases for yearly data.

25. Brady Handgun Control Act, 103rd Cong. (Pub.L. 103-159, 107 Stat. 1536), (1993).

26. John R. Lott Jr., *More Guns, Less Crime: Understanding Crime and Gun Control Laws* (Chicago: University of Chicago Press, 2010), 237 (for a complete statistical analysis of gun control laws and the negative impact they have on the country and local communities).

27. Gary Kleck, *Point Blank: Guns and Violence in America* (Piscataway, NJ: Aldine Transaction, 1991), 47–48.

28. "A Petition Clause Analysis of Suits Against the Government: Implications for Rule 11 Sanctions," 106 Harv. L. Rev. 1111, 1115 (1993).

29. Robert Higgs, *Resurgence of the Warfare State: The Crisis Since 9/11* (Oakland, CA: Independent Institute, 2005). Much of the content for this chapter is inspired by this book, which is both brilliant and provocative in its exploration of the 9/11 crisis.

30. Thomas J. DiLorenzo, *The Real Lincoln: A New Look at Abraham Lincoln, His Agenda, and an Unnecessary War* (Roseville, CA: Prima Lifestyles, 2002), p. 267. DiLorenzo dispels the myths about "Honest Abe" in this truthful and brutal work about Lincoln. He talks about Lincoln's utter disregard for the Constitution; his suspension of *habeas corpus*; his jailing of an opposing U.S. congressman; his true agenda of engaging us in a Civil War in order to advance a political view of centralized, strong, big government. DiLorenzo explains how Lincoln had several options to avoid the Civil War but exercised none of them. He simply could have let the states succeed, as was their constitutional right; eventually, they would have deemed it advantageous to come back to the Union. He also could have compensated slave owners and ended slavery, as did many other countries at that time in history. Every school child should be required to read this account of "Honest Abe."

31. DiLorenzo, "The Great Centralizer: Abraham Lincoln and the War between the States," *The Independent Review,* Fall 1998, Vol. 3, Num. 2, 253, citing Robert Fogel and Stanley Engerman, *Time on the Cross: The Economics of American Negro Slavery* (New York: Norton, 1974), 33–34.

32. DiLorenzo, *The Real Lincoln,* p. 258.

33. Robert Higgs, "If We're Really in Danger, Why Doesn't the Government Act as If We're in Danger?" Independent Institute, October 28, 2002, http://www.independent.org/ newsroom/article.asp?id=114.

34. *Supra* note 29 at 67.

35. Ibid., 24.

36. *Supra* note 29 at 11.

37. Ibid., 10.

38. Ibid.

39. Murray N. Rothbard, *The Case Against the Fed* (Auburn, AL: Ludwig von Mises Institute, 1994).

40. Mike Hewitt, "Ben's Helicopters Are Here!" DollarDaze, December 1, 2008, http://dollardaze.org/ blog/?post_id=00523.

41. Ludwig von Mises, *Theory of Money and Credit* (1912); for a more recent edition, see the 2009 edition (Orlando: Signalman Publishers). Mises explained monetary and banking theory by applying the marginal utility principle to the value of money and then proposing a new theory of industrial fluctuations. Hayek used this as a foundation to build a new theory of the business cycle, which is what later became known as the "Austrian Business Cycle Theory." See Friedrich Hayek, *Prices and Production* (London: G. Routledge, 1931) and Friedrich Hayek, *The Pure Theory of Capital* (London: Macmillan, 1941).

42. US National Debt Clock, http://www.brillig.com/debt_clock/ (accessed August 4, 2010).

43. Source not known.

44. Letter of Thomas Jefferson to William Stephens Smith, 1787.

Other books by Judge Andrew P. Napolitano

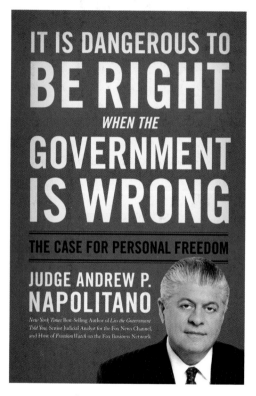

It Is Dangerous to be Right When the Government Is Wrong
The Case for Personal Freedom
978-1-5955-5350-8

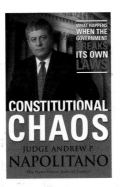

Constitutional Chaos

What Happens When the Government Breaks Its Own Laws

978-0-7852-6083-7

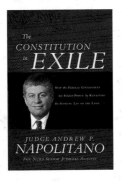

The Constitution in Exile

How the Federal Government Has Seized Power
by Rewriting the Supreme Law of the Land

978-1-5955-5030-9